Poet and Warrior

Balancing your spirit and professional destiny

A human guide for new and aspiring entrepreneurs

Brian J. Dietmeyer

Table of Contents

A Letter to the Reader.. 1

Introduction: Show Me the Data.. 5
Why I wrote this book and how it may apply to you

Getting Ready

**Chapter 1: Who Am I to Leave a Perfectly
Wonderful Life?**...
Permission to reach for your ideal life

Chapter 2: The End Is Where We Start From......................
*A complete and personal redefinition of success
in your life*

Doing It

Chapter 3: Detox..
Purging ourselves of artificial success measurements

Chapter 4: You Want to Own It... It Owns You!...................
*A bias toward positive action and knowing when
to back off*

**Chapter 5: I Never Take Vacations and I Don't Take
Weekends Off**...
*Redefining a life schedule based on your choices,
preferences, and priorities*

Chapter 6: Wise Choices..
*How to make decisions aligned with your own
version of success*

Chapter 7: It's Time to Get a Ph.D.......................................
*Overcoming perceived blocks to goal attainment
and resource allocation*

Chapter 8: Poet and Warrior...
*Coming to terms with a redefined you: balancing
the corporate warrior with your spiritual self*

Getting Better at It

Chapter 9: Success is Meeting Triumph and Disaster and Treating Both Impostors the Same.............................
Maintaining an even keel by being process- versus event-focused

Chapter 10: Sure, It's Easy for You... I Didn't Sleep Last Night!...
Stress management for your new life

Chapter 11: Loving Kindness..
Builds Profit and Brand Equity

Chapter 12: Tie It All Together ....
A review and connection of Chapters 1–11

Chapter 13: Heroes: A Fond Farewell to You, the Reader...
If you're leading your life according to your own personal success measurements, you're a hero

About the Author 91
Your Epitaph 92

A Letter to the Reader

Many years ago, I struggled with my desire to join an investment banking firm or move to the Florida Keys and set up a fruit smoothie operation on the beach! No kidding—I felt a strong draw toward both. I couldn't figure it out; I thought that I must really be screwed up and that I needed to sort things out quickly. My desire for and enjoyment of the electricity and mental challenge of a corporate position ran even with my desire to simplify my life and focus more on the basics—aspects of life that were so enjoyable but seemed out of reach due to the schedule and demands of corporate life. Over and over again, my decision to commit to one or the other flipped and flopped. I was embarrassed: the smoothie operation on the beach sure seemed irresponsible—a dream that was nice to think about but shouldn't be acted upon. I tried to find the answer by asking my friends and family members. Some advised me to "chuck it all—follow your dream!" Others said, "Are you nuts? Leave your corporate career? Nice dream, but not realistic. Take a vacation. Get your head together. Grow up and come back to your job." Neither of these extremes felt right. A sometimes quiet and other times noisy battle raged in me for years. One evening while reading I ran across this Confucian quote:

We can be both poet and warrior.

This quote spoke volumes about the struggle many of us face. Clarity came to me like an explosion. In Western society, we are pressured to be consistent. In fact, in many major companies, there is a strong emphasis on "fitting in." ("This is the way we do things around here, the way we dress, the way we speak to one another in meetings... these are the clubs we belong to, the neighborhoods we live in, the places where we worship...") Sameness is celebrated, and sameness gets you promoted. Originality and self-expression are part of the company mission statement, but only as long as they are within corporate guidelines and culture.

This isn't in and of itself a bad thing, it's just difficult to become who you are in that predefined environment and role. Everything I wanted seemed inconsistent and at odds. The realization that my dreams weren't inconsistent but indicated a need for balance in my life was enlightening and invigorating. I became aware of a wide range of creative opportunities beyond the two obvious choices: either stay employed as a good corporate citizen or become frivolous and "follow my dream." The question is: how can you reach or exceed your potential as a professional warrior while giving equal attention to your inner voice (or poet), whatever that means to you?

It seems to me that this new option is about taking the spiritual revolution of the sixties and the material revolution of the eighties and nineties and finding a spot that is neither "Wall Street investment banker" or "organic bean farmer." This could be the beginning of a complete redefinition-of-success movement for the millennium. In fact, it already is with the huge advent of independent contractors as opposed to employees. We have an opportunity to express ourselves professionally in a manner that exceeds all our earlier work, while paying attention to, nurturing, and not sacrificing our spiritual self. Finding a self-employed way to exceed all of your earlier work in a caring and creative environment is an option. This option is what this book is about. It's about finally saying to yourself: "I can have all that I want, and it is neither irresponsible nor greedy." It's about achieving your human potential your own way, separate from the accepted societal mode. It's about achieving financial and quality-of-life goals simultaneously. It's about being proud of the quality of work you produce and paying attention to a spiritual standard you know is right for you. It's about finding that clarity—whatever is the equivalent of your poet and your warrior. It's about defining what is right for you personally, separate from your age, race, income, social status, etc. It's about defining your own personal measures of success, apart from those society gives us.

Introduction

Show Me the Data

Why I wrote this book and how it may apply to you

The idea of entrepreneurship is celebrated in our country. Why is America so enthralled with entrepreneurs? Because America is a frontier. Ever since the days of the wild, wild west, we've been enamored of the idea of going it alone, breaking new ground, and moving from the known to the unknown. But while we revel in the legend and lore of the frontiers, we also need insight that will help us anticipate the challenges and dangers ahead.

This book is intended to be both a business and human manual for moving from thinking about starting your own business to actually doing it. If you work for a company and are thinking of leaving, this book will give you a glimpse into the future. If you are starting your own business, this book should help you feel less alone and relate to the changes happening in your life.

As corporate managers, we collect data to predict the future so we can make decisions today. This book will give you a sober and accurate picture of the future. It will also offer a sense of "community" for the powerful changes you will experience as you move through the phases of growing your own business.

I wrote this book to fill a void that I experienced before, during, and after my transition. After many years of corporate and academic training, I had learned to search for "data" to aid most of my decisions. I thought that having data would lower my risk, or at least help me decide what to do. I searched for data on what this entrepreneurial thing looked like through the eyes of those who had been through it so I could glimpse the future and lower my perceived risk, but I couldn't find this book anywhere. I was looking for some text that focused on the human aspects of saying goodbye to corporate America.

Many years ago, on a flight to Chicago, I sat next to an entrepreneur. We talked for hours about the differences between having a job and having your own business. At the time, I was working in a Fortune 500 firm and she was a successful entrepreneur working a big Department of Defense contract with the US Navy. Meeting her made me realize that I was attracted to the spirit, energy, caring, and openness of entrepreneurs. At the end of our flight, after much conversation about my nine-year dilemma about leaving corporate life for something more in sync with who I was, she said, "You're not afraid of your ability to survive in an entrepreneurial venture—you're afraid of making the change."

She was right. Very often our confidence in our ability to survive is not the problem; the idea of stripping away all we know, all that had made us successful, all that has defined us for many years, is terrifying.

She suggested a wonderful book called *Transitions* by William Bridges (ironically). Transitions shows you what to expect as you let go of what you know, redefine yourself as you drift in transition, and ultimately reach a more stable place in your new life. Transitions became the guidebook for my life changes. As I read William Bridges' accounts of the human shifts that take place when we join the community of changers, I realized that I was not alone. I was normal. Most of my old contacts still don't understand either what I have done or am thinking of doing, but the stories in this book became the "data" I needed to help me see the future and reduce my own sense of risk.

In my search for insight into the powerful changes I faced as someone both considering and undergoing a corporate life shift, I became increasingly frustrated. Most books were about business planning... or, like Transitions, focused on general life changes. I wanted something that spoke to the droves of people who had left or were thinking about leaving corporate life. I tried to fill the void by organizing a group of entrepreneurs. We began meeting once a month to discuss subjects such as accounting and Internet marketing for small businesses. But we never really talked about the personal issues that kept us awake at night (maybe because this group was almost exclusively male). One night, at dinner after the meeting, I spoke with one of my friends about these issues, issues such as: Do your parents get it? Your friends? Does it feel as if your identity is disappearing? Do you lie awake a night worrying that your idea is a sham and you should go back to being a responsible, corporate adult and just enjoy your job? These were questions I needed answers to, and I couldn't find them in books or meetings with the entrepreneurial group.

Let's go back to the idea of having a job. I strongly believe that the concepts of a "company" and, more importantly, a "job," are made-up models. These models that say we must work a 40- to 60-hour week, climb the ladder, go to meetings, and so on are completely artificial. We accept this all as fact, and we come to see it as the "right" way. I don't dispute that this lifestyle is a good one for many people, but there are other models available.

Early on, we were hunters and gatherers, essentially self-employed people who formed alliances with other self-employed people. We moved on to farming, where we were, in essence, employed by the family business. Up to this point, however, we mostly fended for ourselves or traded what we hunted, grew, or built for other things we needed.

Then came the industrial revolution, and the concept

of jobs was introduced. The connections between what we hunted, what we grew, where we lived, and what we ate were lost. We worked for money, which in turn gave us shelter and food, rather than hunting and growing our own food and building our own shelter. As we began to spend more time away from home, roles and relationships changed radically. As this progressed, many of us moved to two-income households, and finally we began to move our families around the country and around the world. The very fabric that held communities together is challenged by "the corporate move" every 18 months, a move that often means making new friends, being further away from family, and spending more hours away from home. Relationships are hard enough to maintain within our immediate families, let alone with brothers and sisters, aunts and uncles, cousins, and ultimately our network of friends. Yet we accept all this as the norm. Folks, we designed this, and we can change it if it's not working.

The concept of work has evolved radically and will continue to evolve. You are part of that evolution. If you feel out of place in a big company environment, it could be that this current model doesn't fit who you are.

Many times the factors that drive success in big companies don't mesh with the ideals of the individual. Most people who look to start their own businesses dislike many things about the modern organization. Many people who want to start their own businesses have very clear ideas about how they want to work: they are frustrated by the "hoops" and politics in big corporate America and they want to focus more on the work itself. Many times we may feel a subtle or dramatic shift from extrinsic to intrinsic rewards. We want the work to be the reward—not the BMW.

The transition from being motivated by the chance to demonstrate competence to being motivated by the chance to find meaning. It is the shift from the question of how to why.

—William Bridges

Many people are simply tired of making money for someone else. In The Soul's Code, James Hillman says that you don't want to feel as if you're "plodding your way through an already planned map, you are on an itinerary that tells you where you have been before you get there, or like an average statistic foretold by an actuary in an insurance company." For many of us, however, the change keeps getting stalled.

A certain amount of stalling is fine. If there's too much internal "noise" around the decision, better to wait until that noise quiets down and the decision feels more peaceful. On the other hand, there is a point to cut bait, get out, adios, scram.

There are many reasons why people don't make this change. One is the grass-is-always-greener syndrome. When the change seems far away, your job dissatisfaction is high and you dream of the entrepreneurial environment. As you get closer to the dream, the security and comfort of your job begin to look more appealing, and the outside venture looks frightening. Or you're months away from our bonus, or your stock options vesting, or you get promoted.

A friend of mine was a Wall Street type with an M.B.A., very "successful" when he left Wall Street to get a Ph.D. in history. His family thought he was nuts. They started speaking to him softly and slowly. My family was proud of my Fortune 500 vice-president-ness, my money, my success. All the neighbors knew of my accomplishments. When I left, they weren't at all excited—and I'm not certain they "get it" yet.

All of these obstacles are tests to determine your

9

willingness to pursue your dream.

They are early filtering devices that test your entrepreneurial sprit. These attachments will always be there, and when you're ready, you'll have to say goodbye to a lot of things. But the longer you wait, the more there are. I call these things corporate heroin—it's that hard to say goodbye to them, and we need to detox ourselves of them as we transfer to our new role in life. Corporate heroin is unvested stock options, being part of the inner circle, knowing your decisions and the meetings you attend have wide-ranging impact, etc. It is sometimes very difficult to say goodbye to these things. Here's the interesting part: if those things truly aren't important to you personally, they will fade quickly and seem insignificant. On the other hand, if the decision is too "noisy" in your heart, wait until the noise calms down to a dull hum. It'll always be there, but it shouldn't be a roar.

By the way, just because you're dissatisfied doesn't mean you should redefine your life; I believe when you're satisfied you may be better equipped (more on that in Chapter 1).

> *To live a creative life, we must lose our fear of being wrong.*
> —Joseph Chilton Pearce

I am not down on corporate life. I loved it and found it fascinating and rewarding. I'm proud of what I did and I'm proud of my friends who thrive in the corporate environment. Corporations are filled with bright, caring people doing extraordinary things. But let's face it: the corporate model is artificial—it's fiction. A "job" is a made-up entity. The corporate life is merely one option, especially given the liberating nature of technology. You may like your corporate job, you may be good at it, you may even be getting rich at it, but you know in your heart that you need to stop meeting the entrepreneurs and admiring them from afar—you need to become one of them.

When I left the corporate world, another friend, who runs several entrepreneurial ventures in Chicago, said, "Welcome out here with the rest of us." I realized that being the lone wolf doesn't have to be lonely at all. There is a whole other world of people who don't fit the made-up model of a corporate job—working in an office, collecting a paycheck—and this world is growing like wildfire.

I wrote this book to offer you corporate/employed types who are looking for data (beyond business-planning advice) something that will help you glimpse the future and gain insight into the magical and frightening aspects of the entrepreneurial life. I hope this book will also be your guide when you are actually engaged in starting, growing, and managing a small business. I hope it becomes the place you turn to in tough times, a place to help you remember that you're O.K. I want you to proclaim: "Exactly! That's it! I've been there—and it sure is nice to see that others have been as well."

These stories will offer you, the "lone wolf," the opportunity to see yourself in relation to other "lone wolves." This book is about you. Take the time to align the experiences you read about in these pages with yourself, and you'll gain insights into your own transition.

A few words about what this book isn't. It isn't a solution for you. First, I am not qualified to give you a solution. Second, no one but you knows what is right for you. This book chronicles my personal journey, combining stories from my friends, those unrecognized philosophers, with words from some recognized philosophers.

This book is not a how-to book for starting or growing your business through business planning. It's about the "soft stuff" that will guide us as humans in starting or growing our own businesses. It is not full of experts' advice, bit it is filled with real-life, human stories of those who are there with you,

11

challenging you to ask one of the greatest life questions ever: what will make you personally successful in your life?

This isn't a motivational book. I hope that you'll find aspects of it motivational, but this book is really designed to give you an accurate sense of what you can expect to feel during the next phase of your life.

This book is organized into three sections: getting ready for your new life, the first few steps of doing it, and getting better at it. Chapter 1 will speak to the difficulty of making changes if you're mostly happy today. We will then move (in Chapter 2) to determining your personal definition of success, separate from outside influence.

Chapter 3 focuses on ridding ourselves of external success measurements and replacing them with measurements that are more personal to us. Chapter 4 focuses on balancing action, vision, skills, and patience to achieve goals. Chapter 5 will help you shed artificial timelines and schedules in favor of those that are more in line with your preferred life.

In Chapter 6, we'll get serious about making business decisions in an environment where you are no longer separate from the business—you are the business. In Chapter 7, we'll look at how our perceived self-barriers keep us from attaining resources for our businesses or making the shift from a corporate job to self-employment. Chapter 8 will focus on you as both poet and warrior, exploring how you can balance and pay attention to both the spiritual and professional sides of life.

Chapter 9 speaks to facing both success and failure in your new role and finding ways to view them as the same thing. We'll finish with some thoughts on stress management in Chapter 10. Chapters 11 (on loving kindness as a business strategy) and 12 (recap) tie everything together and launch you on your way with a look at the entrepreneur as hero.

Each chapter has exercises designed to move you from broad life goals to personal success measurements, including specific actions to lower stress, make decisions, overcome barriers, and reach your goals, while enjoying the process. I strongly encourage you to attempt the exercises, especially the epitaph exercise.

Is that what they call a vocation, what you do with joy as if you had fire in your heart, the devil in your body?

—Josephine Baker

Chapter 1

Who Am I to Leave a Perfectly Wonderful Life?

Permission to reach for your ideal life

1. You're at your desk. You don't like what you do. You don't like who you report to, and you aren't particularly enamored of the dress code. The commute is too long. That guy in production you deal with every week is getting on your nerves. Your pay raises have been minuscule relative to the mountain of work they keep piling on you. You would love to get out of here and start that business you've always dreamed about.
2. You're at your desk, with a nice view of the fall trees. The new problems that you've just been asked to resolve are right in line with your professional interests. The corporate culture is good; it aligns with your values. Most of the cross-functional team members you deal with have become friends and you look forward to seeing them every day. You feel fairly compensated for your work and find the workload heavy but motivating in its intensity. You like your boss, who is fair but challenges you regularly.

Which of the above people are you? Which one is more likely to redefine him- or herself by making a shift from employee to self-employed? Which one would find the transition easier? More difficult?

Giving Yourself Permission

I found myself in the latter category. I was mostly happy in my life. I wished the company would make it easier for me to leave, help me find something to dislike. Not everything was perfect... it rarely is. But I had no real source of pain to use as a motivation to walk out the door.

It wasn't until many years of wrestling with the decision to leave that two things became apparent. First, it's harder to leave if you're fortunate enough to have a career that is mostly satisfying to you. Things were pretty darn good... good is the enemy of great.

Darrell Connor wrote a book called Managing at the Speed of Change. He tells a story about an oil-rig worker in the North Sea who had always been taught that if a rig catches on fire, you should absolutely not jump into the sea: if the fall doesn't kill you, the burning water or frigid temperatures will. But when the rig caught on fire, this guy jumped—and lived. When asked why—despite of all his training—he jumped, he replied, "Because it was on fire."

When things are mostly good, there isn't a "burning platform" to get us to make a change. We need to realize that at this point we're not escaping something bad, but reaching for a level of true personal success in our life.

The second thing I discovered was a very quiet voice that kept asking, "Who the hell are you to want more?" I had a great job with a respected market leader in an industry that is very creative and a lot of fun. I was well compensated, although my schedule was fairly intense. I realized that I probably would be bored elsewhere. I knew many people within my company and industry who would aspire to be in my position. That quiet voice accused me of being arrogant and self-absorbed because all that, somehow, wasn't enough.

This voice needed to be heard and brought to the forefront in order to give way to a more nurturing voice. This nurturing voice said it was O.K. for me to go after my dreams. It told me that I was doing myself and those I love a disservice by falling short of my personal success measurements. I began to see my job as an ideal link to where I was going, something that gave me the skills I needed to prepare for the transition. I looked deeply and saw that my biggest mistakes and my proudest accomplishments had given me the tools to take the next step. One of your personal key issues may be that all those "wonderful things" that you are lucky to have as part of your existing position actually mean more to other people than to you. Where you are headed should be much more in line with what you value as success.

The following is a passage from *The Artist's Way* by Julia Cameron and Mark Bryan:

Stop telling yourself it's too late.

Stop waiting until you make enough money to do something you really love.

Stop telling yourself "it's just my ego" when you yearn for a more creative life.

Stop telling yourself that dreams don't matter, that they are only dreams and you should be more sensible.

Stop fearing that your family and friends would think you crazy.

Stop telling yourself that creativity is a luxury and that you should be grateful for what you've got.

Every time you don't follow your inner guidance, you feel a loss of energy, loss of power, a sense of spiritual deadness.
— Shakti Gawain

Chapter 2

The End Is Where We Start From

*A complete and personal redefinition
of success in your life*

> *The end is where we start from.*
>
> —T.S. Eliot

I was fortunate enough to enjoy a post-dinner speech one evening by an executive with my former company. This executive asked his audience to write their own epitaphs: what we would really want people to say about our lives after we were gone (not what we thought they were going to say, but what we would like them to say as they looked back and celebrated our lives). At that moment, I realized that we were truly defining life success measurements...and they were zero-based. This exercise had nothing to do with what path we were on, but rather what path we wanted to be on.

As I looked at my epitaph and compared it to my life activity, it became clear that there was a huge disconnect between my life goals and my life activity, yet I was successful and happy... good is the enemy of great.

One of my life goals (that emanated from writing my epitaph) was to believe in myself enough to leave the relative security of a large organization to go out on my own. Notice that this goal spoke to the process of leaving and starting anew, not necessarily the outcome of millions of profit dollars.

Mind you, I have absolutely no problem with getting rich ("Money can't buy you happiness, but it can buy you a big enough yacht to sail right up to it"Johnny Depp), but not if the process of getting there is out of sync with my life goals. I needed to completely zero-base my own definition of success, and this isn't as easy as it appears. I had an awful lot of outside influences on what I deemed as a successful life: What does my family think? What do my friends expect? What does my religion guide us toward? How do my current profession, my current position, and my peers define success? As I looked at my epitaph and analyzed each of these aspects, it occurred to me that many success measurements were being met and having a positive impact on my life, giving me a very good quality of life.

But good is the enemy of great. Good allows us to sub-optimize our life. Good is comfortable; great requires all this redefinition, all this struggling with major life changes. The problem with most of my success measurements is that they were adopted from society rather than custom-built for me from within. As I looked at my new zero-based success measurements (the ones I wanted, not what others believe I should accomplish), it became apparent that I believed myself successful because everyone around me told me I was. When I quit accepting others' success measurements and focused on building my own personal success measurements based on my epitaph, it became apparent that, although some of my "commercial" success was going to assist me in my new direction in life, these accomplishments in and of themselves were not my ultimate success.

Here's the epitaph I wrote that night:

He lived his life simply and with much love.

His home was surrounded by nature and filled with food, wine, and music.

It was a place we came to be with one another:
friends, family, loved ones, and pets.

Based on this, some of my short-term personal bench-
marks or success measurements were:
- Find a place in the country to spend more time
- Cook more for friends and family
- Play the guitar more
- Get a pet

My corporate life had me spending all my time in cities
and airports. I had not communed with nature in years. I was
disconnected from friends and family because of such a hectic
travel schedule. I never found the time to start playing guitar.

A friend had been trying to get me to visit her and her
husband in their home in Connecticut for several years, but
my schedule never allowed it. In a letter to me (written out of
frustration), she wrote, "When you and my husband are 80
years old and looking back on your life, will you remember
the long nights at the office or will you remember the night
you drank too much wine and got lost in the forest collecting
firewood?" This was a simple but strong message for me, one
that made me question early on exactly what success was in
my life, on my terms.

I know many people who have chosen to go out on their
own but have simply carried success measurements with them
from their previous careers. They built in so many familiar
success measurements and situations that they seem to have
merely recreated the same stuff elsewhere instead of writing
the script to fit their own life goals.

We will discover the nature of our particular genius
when we stop trying to conform to our own or to other
peoples' models, learn to be ourselves, and allow our
natural channel to open.

—Shakti Gawain

Think for a moment: what have been the greatest memories of your life in the last six to nine months? Really think about them for a moment: what were the greatest joys and the greatest hassles of your life? Take a close look at the things you truly and simply enjoyed. Any hints on what you need more of in your life?

Let me tell you some of mine: listening to live music, barbequing, being on a very calm lake, water skiing, having friends over for dinner, stripping an old piece of furniture, helping someone think through a problem, watching my nieces and nephews make each other laugh, gardening, going to local stock-car races, seeing a full moon on a warm and windless night, talking with friends and family, having dinner at a local dive.

Some of the hassles: traffic, long meetings that have no apparent purpose, almost any fancy New Year's Eve, almost any five-star restaurant, being on airplanes for three weeks straight. How many times do we need to hear the message we give ourselves after we do something very simple with friends and family? We say, "Man, that was nice—why don't we sit outside more often and talk or play music around a bonfire?" How often do we need to hear age-old sayings like, "It's the simple things in life that make us happy"?

One of my favorite lines from a country song written by Doug Stone is, "Love grows best in little houses." As part of Zen Buddhist precepts in the Korean tradition, your master gives you a name, mine was Mosa, it means humble cottage. He said that a humble cottage has all the comfort without all the stuff, man was he right and man did I ever need to reduce all the noise and overhead to a humble cottage. Think about it. In your job, what are the absolute best parts? What aspects do you love? What parts do you dislike? What parts add to the character of who you are? What parts take away from who you really want to be?

Precision vs. Direction

For many years I wrestled with what the "ideal" life might look like for me. It was sort of like searching for the perfect life partner. There are multiple problems here, the first being that "perfect" is a moving target. What is important to us now may and probably will change in the short and long term. Another difficulty is that many times we haven't "cleared the filter" of all the external noise that defines what is ideal for us, or at least has a very strong influence on the same.

Recently I sat with a Kellogg Graduate School candidate and friend. She was doing extremely well academically, was president of the consulting club, and was actively pursuing the holy grail: a job offer from the Boston Consulting Group or preferably McKinzie. She got the BCG offer. "Why I am not elated?" she asked. This was the prize job as seen by almost everyone in the graduate program, and she had been strongly influenced by this world where she had spent the last two years. But this was not her personal success measurement; it was adopted.

Why do we keep looking for the ideal? Even if we get it, "it" will change. Look for things that are more directional than absolute or precise. Getting on the curve and heading in a direction that is right for you is better than wasting years waiting for the ideal time, opportunity, or circumstance. "Leap and the net will appear" (John Burroughs)...especially if you're leaping toward a destiny that is more appropriate for you. Many entrepreneurs end up in a completely different place than they started. Take a chance at getting on the right path and begin to make decisions that are more right for you personally. Don't worry if your epitaph migrates a bit over time.

KEY POINTS:

Challenge why you may have accepted external success measurements or normal life benchmarks as yours. All the decisions we make in our lives, from the simple to the complex, become much easier if we know where we want to end up. Many times when we are attempting to know what to do, we're driven by the accepted "curve," by the way other people's success measurements have impacted our beliefs. This situation leads to frustration in knowing which job to choose, how many hours to work, when to vacation, which person to marry. You need to decide what is right for your life, how you want this gift of life to be spent, then set some short-term success measurements or benchmarks along the way. You are the only one who knows if you're successful or not. No one else can tell you what success looks like.

Please turn to the very last page of this book and write your epitaph. Take your time—this could and should be life-changing!

To know what you prefer instead of humbly saying Amen to what the world tells you you ought to prefer, is to have kept your soul alive.

—Robert Louis Stevenson

Chapter 3

Detox

*Purging ourselves of
artificial success measurements*

I want to tell you a very personal story to either prepare you for what may be happening or what will happen as you shed the old you and the new you begins to show up. For 17 years, I had worked for the same company, slowly working from an hourly-wage position to the corporate-level management team. I worked 6–7 days a week and 10–12 hours a day for a good period of that time. I traveled at least 100,000 miles each year and spent 3–4 nights every week away from home. I was having a blast, making good money, and developing friendships with many people in my company and my industry. In fact, nearly 100% of the kid who left the South Side of Chicago had slowly slipped away as I traded up for a more affluent lifestyle and made many new friends. Long gone were the days of drinking beer with my pals, hanging around the lake on weekends, having barbeques, driving hot rods and motorcycles, and going to hear live music.

My life, who my friends were, where my power came from, my very definition—all these things were tied to being a guy with a big job working for a big company. It was the way I was introduced to people. This new lifestyle, friends, vocabulary, travel schedule, moving from Chicago to Tucson to Phoenix to Santa Barbara made it difficult to separate my company, my title, and my job from me. When I met people, they either wanted something from me (such as a job) or I needed something from them (they were a boss, client, or employee). It never seemed that people would just show up for who they were at corporate events (and most of my life was a version of a corporate event). It seemed that even in leisure time (at bowling alleys, having dinner parties, etc.) there was always an employee, a boss, a customer or potential customer involved.

So now you get the picture: for half my life, I had been slowly defined by the company I worked for, and I had accepted its rules and success measurements. Once again, please keep in mind that by most measurements (except my own), I was very successful (although I definitely wasn't miserable... good is the enemy of great). But I digress...all this build-up is to set the stage for what happened next. I lost:
- my job
- my house
- my car
- my girlfriend
- most of my worldly possessions
- most of my friends/relationships
- my paycheck.

I decided to leave corporate life to start my own company. There went the paycheck, some friends (alleged friends!), and of course my job with its title, responsibilities, all the important meetings where my attendance was mandatory and made me seem important. Since my income was to be limited as I started a business, I decided to sell my fancy loft in favor of a small, multiple-unit investment property, where I could act as landlord and lower my monthly expenses. I was also going to act as general contractor on the remodeling of the building.

Well, the remodeling took twice as long (and twice as much) as I thought. I had sold my house and had to put my stuff in storage. I stayed with my girlfriend until I irritated her enough that she booted me out; then I had to rent a place month to month with most of my stuff still in storage. I came out one morning to discover that my car had been stolen (city living!). So there I was, driving a rental car, with none of my own stuff, no job to go to, no house of my own, no girlfriend, and no paycheck. Saying my life went from being structured, defined, planned, and decided to being absolutely, positively, completely untethered in every sense is the wildest under-statement I could make! At that point, I was neither what I had been or what I would become. My new company was nothing more than an idea, so I couldn't be defined by that. Most of my familiar furniture, my car, and my house were all gone. The only thing left was me and a lot of silence. It was scary and rich and awesome. It was the first time I had spent time with myself in a while, and it was difficult since I wasn't sure who I really was at that point.

In a similar situation, your first reaction might be to want to run back to some familiar comfort as soon as possible. But I say: lace up your boots a little tighter, pull that seatbelt low and snug across your lap, and enjoy the ride! Everything will be more defined soon enough. Allow the germ of who you really are to grow and emerge. You may eventually rekindle portions of your old life, but at least you'll be doing it proac-tively and by choice. Take as much time as you can to detox from your old life. For me, it took about a year before things felt a bit more "normal." My new "normal," however, looked very different from my old "normal." But the new one is mine by design, for better or for worse—it ain't perfect, but it's mine.

As my old definitions of success were taken from me by storm, new definitions began to emerge. I kept thinking about what would happen if my business didn't work and I lost valuable time on the "power curve" by being away from corporate America—not to mention the loss of money. When

I thought about these things, my decision seemed very risky to me. But a very funny thing happened as I began to make changes in my life: I reversed out of societal success measurements to measurements that were more personal to me. I looked at my epitaph and realized that one of my life dreams was to have the courage to let go of the apron strings of having a job and go out and try it on my own. My goal was to find out how much of my success was tied to the company where I had worked for 17 years and how much was me. Given that, take a look at this logic: if I had stayed in corporate America, there was a 100% chance I would be unsuccessful (according to my own personal success measurements). Does that make sense? No matter how much power I attained and how much money I made, if my goal was to have the confidence to go out and try, I would be successful just by doing it! By leaving and starting my own company, I had achieved success the moment I walked out the door, even if I had to come back begging for a job one day.

This redefinition of success also completely defined risk. Now, risk is looking forward to my last days and saying, "Well, I made it to president of a public company, earned millions and never had the guts to live my life in a way specifically designed for me. I was successful by many standards, but not by my own personal ones." If, on my deathbed, I realize that I only achieved 30% of my earnings capacity over my life but had the courage to do things the way I wanted (at no expense to others) and designed my life work and life schedule, I will have been a success. For me, it was riskier to stay in corporate America than to leave, because if I stayed my dream would never be achieved. It was time to go.

Chapter 4

You Want to Own It... It Owns You!

*A bias toward positive action
and knowing when to back off*

How do we get some momentum moving on our new idea or new company or new passion, however we define it? Let me start with this: the sooner we realize that everything is leased, the easier all this stuff gets. Everything is leased... especially magic. Affairs of the heart, special moments, all the times when we "want it to be this way forever." We learn from jujitsu the concept of working with the opposing force. If an attacker comes at us, we can either back up a few steps, build some forward momentum, then hit him head on, or we can merely wait until he gets close enough, step aside, and let him fall forward on his own.

My friend and backyard philosopher said about relationships, "As soon as you want to own it, it owns you." As he spoke of his own relationship, his outlook was that his relationship was good—better than most—but he didn't try to hold on to it, make it stay the same forever. He said, "I'm grateful for every day I get. Each day is wonderful, and I cherish it for what it is. If she leaves me tomorrow, I won't be happy, but I'll accept it. I'm focusing on what I have right now and enjoying it."

If you really want it, back off, relax, let it go. Let it come to you. Obsessing about it may drive it away.

Let's say you're waiting on a decision for a huge contract,

29

a new person to join your firm, an O.K. from an alliance, approval from a bank, investment capital. You can stay awake at night and obsess, or do what you can and back off, relax, let it come to you. I cannot count the number of times when something showed up the moment I quit obsessing about it.

Where does hard work fit into all this? How about positive imagery? The power of positive thinking? Where does all this stuff fit? How do we make things happen? It seems to be a combination of art and science, a balance of yin and yang. One thing I know for sure is that it is difference from how we make things happen in a "job."

First, you have to want it.

Second, you have to supplement technical skills.

Third, take action to get there.

Fourth, chill.

You Have To Want It

You gotta want it. Say it any way you want: visual imagery, positive thinking, sending out your intent, alerting the universe, praying to God. Just want it. See it. Picture yourself in it. Know it's working. See, think, and feel the details of your new or improved venture. Write it down: in the back of your journal, anywhere. You have to believe that your thoughts drive your actions, drive your results.

Most people I know subscribe to the notion of positive thinking, whether they're old-school Christians or New Agers. What I tend to see hear less about is the idea that we also attract our greatest fears. What we think negatively also drives our actions, drives our results. If we think we will lose the deal, lose money, have difficulties, we will find a way to make all these things happen. If we think that we'll be world-class, have a blast in our new venture, the new alliance will do well, we will also find a way to make these things happen. It's interesting to me that most of us understand, accept, and even practice the concept of positive visualization, but we fail to realize that we also attract our greatest fears. What we think drives our actions, drives our results.

The lesson in all such experiences is that when we are ready to make a beginning, we will shortly find an opportunity.

—William Bridges

One thing to keep in mind is to see it yourself. Avoid falling into the trap of looking for too much confirmation for your idea. First, any idea you have is yours. By and large it succeeds because of you, not the business plan, not the niche it fills, not how well-financed it is. Many poor ideas have been financially successful only because of the drive, caring, and commitment of their founders. Likewise, many well-funded, niche-perfect concepts have died because of the knucklehead at the helm.

Second, if it's expert advice you want, go get it—but remember, it's just a tool. Stop and ask: is it advice you want, or approval? Very few people who are stuck in ruts or not interested in self-definition will welcome and support your idea with open arms. Alas, it's time to begin acting like an entrepreneur and find that resolution in your own heart. It's now your job to convince others...not to be convinced.

Learning to Play the Guitar

Not until I quit learning to play the guitar did I begin to play. For many months, I said, "I'm learning to play the guitar." But when do you quit learning and start playing? You start playing instantly. You don't play well by popular

31

standards instantly, but you play your finest two chords to the best of your ability instantly.

Another friend and spiritual mentor schooled me on making my business world-class. Early on, working from my kitchen table, my business plan stated a very clear objective: the firm, however small or large, would be world-class in the truest sense of the word. Not a corporate buzzword or a drive-by mission statement, but the benchmark in the world for our particular skill.

This was a lofty and long-term goal. As my intern and I sat at the kitchen table with faithful Jahno (a 110-lb Rottweiler) obsessing along with us, it seemed like a lot more money, customers, and time in the market would lead us toward becoming world-class. But my friend and intern, as he is wont to do, knocked me out of my chair with a very simple statement: "World class begins today, Tuesday, at 9:43 a.m., complete with Rottweiler drool on our printer. Every phone call we make and answer, every fax, every e-mail, every letter we send will be world-class immediately." We stopped working on becoming world-class and started being world-class, one transaction at a time. Everything we did ran through that filter and that standard.

Theory of Abundance

When we meet homeless people on the street, do we give them money? Not even a question: absolutely, positively. We have money to give. We have more than our brother and sisters on the street. Invest in them. Invest in yourself. We are all connected. Giving to others is not that at all; there is no other and no self. We give to humanity. We are all a part of the same humanity.

Native Americans say that "life eats life." We die, we go into the ground, we fertilize the earth, plants draw from our energy, animals draw energy from the plants, we in turn draw energy from the animals and plants, and on goes the cycle ad infinitum. Do we invest in our business? Absolutely, yes. We are investing in ourselves. We "act as if" and it will be.

Don't portray your venture as young and starving; portray your venture as healthy and growing. Spend the extra effort, heart, and capital. It will come back. Do it willfully and do it responsibly, do it with utmost confidence, expecting a 100% return.

I learned the concept of "acting as if" from a therapist many years ago. Even if you're not there yet, believe it—act as if today. If you want others around you to believe in your idea, you must believe in it first—others will catch on. I am not thinking about writing this book, I am not learning what it is to write the book, I am writing the book to the absolute best of my own personal ability at this moment. No more. No less. Your thoughts and attitudes about what your new venture will be and how it will be begin in your mind and your heart and are proven by your actions and decisions.

Go confidently in the direction of your dreams! Live the life you've imagined. As you simplify your life, the laws of the universe will be simpler.

—Henry David Thoreau

You Have To Supplement Technical Skills

Here comes the science of the art-and-science side. No amount of wanting, visualizing, or positive thinking can supplement a lack of technical skills. Remember the old saying that knowing what you're good at is important, but knowing your weakness is even more important. Naturally, as an existing or would-be entrepreneur, you have very strong skills in many general areas and a few specific ones. My weakness is accounting. As an entrepreneur, do I need to "do everything"? Absolutely not! Early on, my partner and I realized that I was good in marketing communications and training delivery and had a strong intuitive sense of how to build training programs (instructional design). This skill is fundamental to designing training programs for corporate clients. It wasn't enough to have a good intuitive sense; we needed hard-core technical skills here, so we found a way to supplement our own abilities.

Determine your strengths and weaknesses. If any of your weaknesses are key to success in your business, find a way to beg, borrow, buy, or rent what you lack—don't let your ego get in the way. Your job as an entrepreneur is not to do it all, but to manage getting it done in the most efficient and effective way possible. Target and improve your strengths and go after your weaknesses with a vengeance. Find a way to remedy them—if you don't, the market will quickly and painfully let you know what they are. Recently, I have been fortunate enough to take on several new partners in my firm, all of them, to a person have many strengths greater than mine. The liberation that occurs from seeing an initial idea that I had either squashed because it was way off base or made 5 times better due to their input is powerful and motivating.

Take Positive Action, Not Just Any Action

Another friend really helped me understand the whole idea between leading and lagging indicators. Jon pointed out that most sales managers and general managers claim to be "involved in the sales process," when in fact they are auditors of the sales process. We meet with the salespeople and review goals and actual results and are therefore active participants. My friend argues that effective managers focus on the things that lead to success instead of on success.

When Mike Ditka was coach of the Chicago Bears, I remember an interview in which he was asked about which players were earning what kind of money. He pointed out that the guys who were focusing on and complaining about their salaries were making less than the guys who practiced and played their hearts out. The players with an intense focus on the leading indicators (headlights) ultimately found great success when it came time for lagging indicators (taillights).

Now that you have a clear view of where you want to go and some idea of your own personal success measurements, you need to think about which activities are most likely to get you where you want to be. As an entrepreneur, your time needs to be focused on what you like doing that will ultimately lead you to where you are going. Put your limited time and action against those things that have the highest probability of getting you closest to your personal success measurement.

I have not worried as much about generating sales as I have worried about making our product better and better. A great product will find sales through referrals and reputation. I want a lot of sales eventually and am very clear that job number one is a quality training and adoption process (in my business—what is it for yours?); 90% of my energy goes toward training, product development, and delivery, sustaining etc. Only when those things feel tight will I worry about high-volume sales. I think Bill Marriott, Sr. (of Marriott Hotels) was right many years ago when he said, "Take care of your employees, take care of your customers, and profits will take care of themselves." I also remember a friend saying, "You're putting an addition on your house when the foundation's on fire." She made a great and painful point. Make sure that you have a strong bias toward action: the right action, the leading indictors, the process steps that lead to your personal success measurements.

...stop getting ready and act. Getting ready can turn out to be an endless task, and one of the forms inner resistance often takes is the attempt to make just a few more preparations.

—William Bridges

Chill

Are you a U2 fan? How about Nirvana? How long do you think these musicians played in garages, at parties, and in small clubs before their music "took off overnight"? Most famous people will say over and over again that they were not overnight successes—in fact they worked for years molding and reworking their craft, playing to small audiences, and just getting by.

My business has been the same. After a very slow start and years of hammering away, things began to improve rapidly. Seventeen years of corporate experience, undergraduate and graduate degrees (the latter earned over 10 years of night school), combined with my partner's 20 years of teaching experience at Harvard and elsewhere—all this in addition to years in our new venture trying to break in, knowing we had a better product all the time. Nothing but patience and "time in grade" earned us respect and breakthroughs.

If you're like me (and most of my friends running new businesses), you wonder when you'll lose your confidence and begin to question your concept, your ideas, your skills. Keep hammering, keep getting better, keep making contacts—and relax, enjoy the process, allow it to happen. This might seem like a slight difference from making it happen, but it will mean a world of difference in your attitude and perspective. Let go of "where you're going" and "when you'll get there" and focus on what you're doing right now. As Buddhists are fond of saying, "when washing the dishes, just wash the dishes."

You may also notice people hanging around the periphery, waiting for you to be successful. It's sort of like the bank that will not loan you money when you need it, but will loan it to you when you're successful and you no longer need it. People, opportunities, and clients are all waiting for some modicum of success, and you may feel frustrated. We tend to want too much too soon. Have a clear vision, supplement what you need, work hard, and then allow your patience to be a clear action step in your plan. Relax and let it work for you. Those who will not quite commit as they await your success today will be still there tomorrow, wanting to be associated with your venture as the "ball of energy" around what you are doing grows.

I offered a very lucrative opportunity to a promising young talent early on, and he said, "I'll be ready in a few years." Translation: "I'll be ready when this thing shows promise." I told him that the reward I was ready to offer him today will not be the same one year from now when the risk is lower.

We have to be patient and know that, in time—and at the right time—we'll gain access to what we want. If you've ever worked on a car or motorcycle, you know that you can work for hours trying to get a new part to bolt onto where it's supposed to go. Many times the best thing you can do to get it to bolt on is to walk away (my brother's advice). It's amazing: when you come back to it the next day, it slips right on. I can't count how many times I "walked away" from something in my business after obsessing over making the thing happen, only to have it happen the moment I let it go.

Add relaxing and sitting back to your list of "action" steps when you're trying to get something done. And remember: when you want to own it, it owns you!

KEY POINTS:

Combine clear visualization, positive reinforcing thought, an objective review, and supplementation of key skills with actions designed with a specific purpose in mind. Cultivate a sense of when you've done enough to back off. This balanced plan or blueprint with make and allow things to happen in your new venture. See your future and begin accomplishing it in the present.

EXERCISES:

- Is your vision really clear to you? Describe it in detail.
- What are your strengths?
- What are your weaknesses?
- What, specifically, can you do to shore up these weaknesses?
- At this point in your process, what are the key activities that will lead to actualization of your vision?

Chapter 5

I Never Take Vacations and
I Don't Take Weekends Off

*Redefining a life schedule based on
your choices, preferences, and priorities*

Who came up with the concepts of weekday and weekend? Where did the concept of working vs. vacation or holiday time originate? I absolutely refuse to take weekends off. Even more so, I refuse to take my two weeks in the Caribbean in the winter and one week by the lake in the summer. I refuse to work an 8- or 9-hour day.

Much like the concept of a job or a work week, holidays and weekends are human inventions that we can also redefine. When did it become appropriate to compartmentalize our lives in such a way that there is even a distinction between work and play? The entrepreneur's role is to redefine these distinctions.

When I first went out on my own, I promised myself that I would become very task-oriented. I start the day or week with a certain amount of things I want to accomplish: make three new customer contacts, follow up on five outstanding customers, deliver a two-day training session, clean up the accounting, write the second module for an upcoming training. If all this takes me 70 hours to do, so be it. If it takes a Saturday or Sunday, so be that as well. On the other hand, I may choose to work 12 hours a day Saturday through Monday and take Tuesday and Wednesday off to ski because the weather is clear and the lake is calm. So be it.

As an entrepreneur, you have to keep the business going at a level that speaks to your personal success measurements. And I mean your personal success measurements in total—not just a race to build up your lifestyle to the new level of income, then continue to add more money and more stuff. Your success measurements include income, lifestyle, personal goals, and the type of balanced and multidimensional life you've been seeking. Your business is not a job where 40 hours is the expected work week and any more time means you're either getting taken advantage of or building points with the boss, and any less time means you could get fired. You own this. It may take 80 hours, or it may take 20 hours this week. The current standard of 40–50 hours has been convenient as a convention for most, but it's no longer appropriate for you.

In statistics, most of us learned the concept of a standard normal curve: all random events follow a pattern that is somewhat predictable. Statistics that say 80% of us are married by 25, have one child by 27 and two by 30, and so on have helped develop the work week. They define fashion, "appropriate behaviors," our careers, job titles, incomes, and a host of other measurable life benchmarks. Here's the rub: many of us allow where we are on the "curve" to direct our behavior. We use the curve to gauge our success. Everyone else's behavior literally defines what we see as success. The crazy part is that most people I know are dissatisfied with these generally accepted standards but still work like dogs to exceed them!

As an entrepreneur, you'll find that your ability (or desire, for that matter) to maintain equilibrium with the curve will be completely out of whack. Once you get comfortable with this fact, the external and internal pressures to conform to the curve dissipate considerably. Build your own curve! You're the only one with a benchmark that is appropriate. This may take a bit of negotiation with your loved ones, but it's worth it.

I will not argue for nonconformity for its own sake, but neither will I argue for acceptance of the curve as fact. You have the only clock. You set the only benchmark. By benchmarking the "best in class" at any particular part of your life, you run the risk of severely limiting where you can go and how full your life can be—you can completely redefine the accepted norm for that part of your life. If you accept the best benchmark "out there" as your goal, you could be completely capable of a fundamental redefinition of what success means in a particular category of life.

Best does not always mean the biggest, fastest, most. Let's take vacations, for example. I never take them—but last year I went to the Florida Keys, Barbados, Tucson, and South Beach in Miami. None of these were vacations and none of them were business trips—they just were where I was at the time.

The separations between what I do and who I am, when I work and when I play, weekday and weekend, workday and holiday have become very fuzzy. Have you ever noticed the huge letdown you feel toward the end of a vacation as you realize it's back to work for the next 6–12 months? I never have that letdown anymore. I spent a week in the Florida Keys and worked each morning until noon. I went to the beach for a couple of hours, came home, had lunch, worked out, and then worked again—sometimes before and after dinner. Was this work or vacation?

Many career options today give you this flexibility, allowing you to redefine a lifestyle that is most appropriate for your idea of life success... not what is most common (albeit completely synthetic). The line from the Desiderata that states we should "never compare ourselves with others for we will only become vain and bitter" helps guide me here.

There is also a great book called The Millionaire Next Door by Thomas J. Stanley and William D. Danko. Shortly after the book's release, 48 HOURS featured many of these "millionaires next door." One of my favorite comments (and a common thread throughout the program) came from a real estate millionaire who lived as if he were making $40,000 per year: no fancy car, no Armani suits, no spectacular house. When asked how he was enjoying the fruits of his labors, he replied, "I fished 100 days last year." Last time I checked, I didn't see that benchmark on most "standard normal curves" for the American dream. It was the dream for that particular human. (By the way, he was wildly successful if his goal was to fish 50 days last year.) Can you imagine a Fortune 100 list of people who had fished the most days last year, with this guy's picture on the cover?

This millionaire also told a story of being in the bank one Friday. The teller said, "Aren't you glad it's Friday and the work week is over?" The millionaire replied, "No, I like Mondays—the river is less crowded."

It's all about defining what is right for you, and it can begin with your life success measurements or your epitaph. Begin with the end in mind.

Chapter 6

Wise Choices

*How To Make Decisions Aligned
With Your Own Version of Success*

Indecision may or not be my problem...

—Jimmy Buffett

Let's face it: success in your new life is nothing more than a compilation of rational decisions. For our purposes, "rational decisions" will be defined as those made in accordance with our own epitaphs and personal success measurements.

Decisions made in the corporate environment are complex but easy. In the entrepreneurial environment, the separation between the business and you is almost invisible, so how do you stay balanced and rational when making decisions that are highly personal and professional?

Once I made the decision to leave my corporate career, I had to decide what to do as my business. My two choices were a restaurant/bar or a training/consulting business. For awhile, the restaurant/bar was clearly winning: it offered so much creative freedom and none of the typical constraints of corporate life. I could finally grow my hair back! In the restaurant/bar business, creativity and individuality are accepted and rewarded. This environment seemed much more in line with my epitaph and personal success measurements.

The bar was to be called D'Amico's. When I was young,

43

I lived on the South Side of Chicago. My older sister Nancy dated a very cool guy by the name of Coz D'Amico. Coz (short for Cosmo) played football at Leo High School, a Catholic, all-boys school. He was my idol. We used to go the football games at Soldier Field in Chicago. This guy was the best. He was like a movie star to me. He and my sister used to drag me out on dates when she baby-sat me, and wherever we went I remember hearing Motown/R&B music.

Chicago is divided into two main sections: the North Side (Cubs/white collar) and the South Side (Sox/blue collar). I now live on the North Side, and I still long for the South Side color. In fact, many of my South Side pals now live here. D'Amico's was going to be a place for us: a dark little tavern with blacked-out windows, a pool table, Slim Jims, pickled pigs' feet and eggs, lots of Motown music, south side high-school yearbook pictures on the walls. When I thought about D'Amico's, my excitement ran at an all-time high. The other option—the training and consulting business—would keep me in a corporate haircut, suit, and all the other corporate constraints.

Decision-making is an elegant blend of art and science, balancing what we feel with logic and linear thought. Market research tells us to start designing our questions with the answers in mind. Do we choose how to live our life and reason backward?

The epitaph exercise was the best one I ever did. My life was incongruent with my ultimate goals (a house, food, music, critters, quiet). I sat back and thought about the training I had received in business school about making decisions, especially personal ones like this. It's hard to remain objective when making any decision, even more so when you're an entrepreneur without an infrastructure to temper your emotions. As an entrepreneur, the business is yours and therefore more personal: you're a lot more vulnerable to non-rational decision-making.

44

As I thought through the decision process, I tried to define the important elements:
- What criteria should I use to evaluate both alternatives (consulting vs. bar business)?
- Which of those criteria are most and least important?
- How do each of these alternatives score against each weighted criterion?
- On average, which is the better decision?

Talk about a bucket of cold water! My criteria were creativity, income, intellectual challenge, portability, and low risk/capital investment. Two of my most important criteria were the ability to work from almost anywhere (portability) and low capital risk. Needless to say, the bar did not score very well on the important criteria of low capital risk and portability. My own emotions around the creativity criterion were so loud they were drowning out everything else. When I analyzed the situation, I realized that, on average, the consulting/training business met my overall needs about 200% better than the bar.

In a letter dated in the 1700s to a scientist friend, Ben Franklin said two things:
1. I can't tell you what decision to make, but I can advise you on how to make a better decision.
2. The problem with making decisions is that all the reasons pro and con are not present in the mind at the same time.

No one could have helped me make this decision, since my long-term goal (epitaph) drove my short-term goal (personal success measurement), which in turn drove the criteria and weighting for this decision. Steven Covey is fond of saying that we need to align "what we think, what we feel, what we say to achieve our own true North." Where we personally want to end up should be aligned with our own shorter-term

45

benchmarks, and this alignment should assist us in day-to-day decision-making.

The criteria and weighting you use for making decisions are uniquely yours, based on what success looks like for you. The more decisions you make with criteria that are aligned with your own "true North," the sooner your life will begin to look like yours instead of a conglomeration of others' beliefs, desires, and rules.

As an existing or new entrepreneur, you are now the fundamental decision-maker. No one else can make these decisions for you. Only you know where you want to go. Others can and should, however, play important roles in discussing, challenging, and reviewing which criteria should be used to evaluate choices (which are most to least important, how the alternatives score against these criteria, and so on).

The risk is that these decisions are so personal that you need to take more of a process-oriented approach to factor out inappropriate emotions. You need emotion and, more importantly, energy to run and grow your own business; what you don't need is emotion run amok. This will bias your decisions in ways that are detrimental to where you want to go. Ben Franklin couldn't tell his friend which decision to make, but he could help him make the decision, which is where this process leads us and where we have to be as entrepreneurs.

Franklin's other comment had to do with all the criteria and weighting not being present in the mind at the same time. This was my problem with D'Amico's. One criterion—creativity—was scoring so high and screaming so loudly at me that I couldn't even hear the other criteria through my desire to finally be able to go to work in a ponytail!

...life is a moment by moment choice between safety (out of fear and need for defense) and risk (for the sake of progress and growth).

—Satori Now, Awakening your Highest Self,
David Tuffley

Try the exercise at the end of this chapter. I promise you that just identifying criteria will improve your decision process immediately.

If any of this sounds too analytical, allow me to share some thoughts from Money Choices by Max Bazerman, Ph.D. (my partner). Max's book has a great section on the struggle between the "should" self and the "want" self. Here's an example: you're heading home from work. The "should" self nags, "Let's go to the gym. You know you should. It's good for you physically and reduces stress." The "want" self says, "I want to go home, watch a video, order a pizza, and have a beer." Which self is right? ("I should stay with my job, but I want to start my own business.") The "should" self tends to be more focused on the long term.

The "should" self sounds a lot more mature and focused on long-term benefits, but the "want" self also plays a significant role. For example, when we get hungry, we want food. Hunger is a good metaphor for any "want" that is or could be important to us. Max argues that the approach to decision-making outlined in this chapter and in the following exercise "would most likely favor the 'should' self, but would give voice, opportunity, and input to the 'want' self."

KEY POINTS:

Making rational decisions doesn't mean we take out the human factor. In fact, if rational decision-making is defined as seeking decisions that are "in our best interests," then they

47

are the most human of all decisions. Where you want to go in your life should drive your daily decisions. The decisions you make each day are mostly tactical, and they need to factor in your life strategy (epitaph/personal success measurements).

EXERCISES:

- What critical decision/choice are you facing as it relates to starting or growing your business (i.e., leaving corporate life)?
- What are your options/alternatives (i.e., restaurant/bar vs. consulting business)?
- Which criteria are most (1) to least (5) important in making this decision? (Make every attempt to choose these criteria based on your epitaph and personal success measurements, not what everyone else would choose as important criteria for your decisions.)
  1.
  2.
  3.
  4.
  5.
- Allocate points (0–100) to each criterion as it relates to that alternative.
  Alternative 1 (points)
  Alternative 2 (points)
  1.
  2.
  3.
  4.
  5.
- Which alternative, on average, is the better one for you?

Chapter 7

It's Time to Get a Ph.D.

Overcoming perceived blocks to
goal attainment and resource allocation

In a meeting with a major client, my partner and I were discussing our backgrounds and how we met. (I was participating in the Executive MBA program at Kellogg and Max was a professor there.) During the course of the conversation, our client asked me if I'd ever thought about getting a Ph.D. I pointed to Max and said, "I got one."

In starting a training or consulting business, it helps immensely to be published and to have a Ph.D. Going back to school and then starting a business would have put me way behind in my personal life schedule. It seemed impossible to invest that many years and that much money (while not working) into getting a Ph.D.

The perceived barrier of obtaining a Ph.D. could have easily derailed my dream of starting a consulting and training business. But when I looked at redefining my problem as "How can my business obtain the benefits and credibility of a Ph.D.?" things got easier. Thinking "I need a Ph.D." is fairly limiting. Asking "Why do I need a Ph.D.?" is much more liberating. The answers were more credibility for me and cutting-edge research and processes for my customers. I realized there were many options for "getting a Ph.D.": I could hire one, I could share equity with one, I could create an alliance with one, or I could go back to school and get one myself. Redefining the problem by focusing on the underlying reason (why I needed a Ph.D.), I discovered multiple ways to achieve what the business needed.

Soon after I did this creative exercise, I did a financial analysis of my different options. Obtaining my own Ph.D. involved several cash flows: the cost of an education, loss of revenues while I was out of market, and the opportunity cost of missing four years of climbing the learning curve and developing clients and my product. The trade-off of offering my partner equity and cash flows relative to the total alternative of obtaining my own Ph.D. was an easy decision.

As the business neared the end of its first year, we faced a challenge. My time was being spread thin between sales, product development, and product delivery, and I realized that I was beginning to do most things on a suboptimal basis How could I hire someone to do some of these things? I needed a salesperson, since I was the only one who could focus on content and delivery. But there was a problem: cash flow. We couldn't afford a salesperson, let alone a sales force. I had hit a roadblock.

I got around this roadblock by redefining the problem. I moved from "How do I hire a salesperson?" to "How do I find a way to generate more sales and free up some time for product development?" Given this problem, I could see many solutions. We ended up developing an alliance with a consulting firm that had a sales force of 15 people and complementary products and processes to ours. We now had mind-share of 15 people selling our products with very low risk. We had no capital outlay and only paid when sales were closed. We also enhanced our credibility by aligning with an established firm that had a strong reputation.

The entire concept of starting a business begins with a very large roadblock called "risk." The risk of personal failure, the risk of losing money that would be invested in the business, the risk of losing valuable time moving up the corporate power curve. If you find yourself stopped by these roadblocks, it's time to rethink the problem. What is actually at risk here? This begs the question of what will make you successful. "Success" is precisely what is at risk.

My (dearly departed) brother Dan was an old school biker, race car driver and mechanic, among other things. When we were teens and building our first stock car for Raceway Park in Chicago, I noticed we didn't have a roll cage and all the other cars didn't. We didn't have the time or the money to install one. I however felt compelled to point this out to Dan who said, "roll cages are for sissy's and smart people and we ain't neither!". It's a definition of risk management I don't necessarily agree with but needed to get his quote in the book!

At this point, for me, it became riskier to stay in my job, because there was a 100% probability that I would not reach "success" if I stayed employed, and a 100% probability I would reach "success" if I left and started a business. The real risk was looking back at the end of my life and regretting never having taken the chance. And I knew that regret would not have been lessened by having a larger pile of assets than the person next door.

An ideal way to get past roadblocks is to borrow an exercise from Eastern philosophy: "Ask five times why." Try it sometime. If you really want something, ask yourself why you want it. Then ask again, why is that important and again, and so on. You may find alternate ways to solve your problem—or you may realize that you no longer need the thing at all.

My personal belief is that there are many motivational speakers out there who claim that once you're on the "right path" for yourself, there are "unseen hands" that help you along. I want to add a bit of my own theory to this… the universe also tests you. I have seen this again and again. Answers are never black and white, the right path to take it not crystal clear, the world is gray, it is the middle way. When ever I have pursued something of importance to me, there seem to be initial signs that point that I've made the right decision, then, WHAM! An obstacle or two come in my way. it seems to me that the bigger the challenge or change you are undertaking, the larger test the universe will send your way. Here is the rub, too many tests, too much noise about the decision sometimes, we need to walk away. On the other hand, if you really want it, punch thru that wall and then, for the most part, you will feel that unseen hand helping you along. It is being conscious enough to recognize the test to see if you really want that next step or the universe screaming to change paths again.

No amount of skillful invention can replace the essential element of imagination.

—Edward Hopper

Invest In Yourself

Many people I speak with are frustrated by their lack of resources to start or advance their businesses. Often we may be frustrated because we don't think we have enough resources, but at the same time we're sitting on real estate or equity market investments we view as untouchable. These investments should be an integral part of your strategy to find capital to start or grow your business.

Money invested in the market is by and large completely out of your control. The money is managed by a broker or fund manager and invested in companies that are run by a management team you will probably never meet. Our investments have treated us well in the past, even with their ups and downs. As a potential or new entrepreneur, look at your business as simply one more way to invest and to diversify your portfolio. What better place to invest than you? And if you want others to invest in your business, are you prepared to do the same?

Some analysts would tell you to invest others' money and keep your own assets protected from risk. This is a reasonable argument. But think about it this way: what is a better investment, you and your idea or the equity or real estate market? Challenging your assumptions in this area may bring to light a fresh way to consider the risk of your business plan. What needs to change in your plan to make you comfortable enough to risk your personal "sacred fund"? My business, my rental properties, this book, and my mutual fund investments are all part of my total net worth. As I look at where my time is invested, where my money is invested, where all resources are directed, I can see that they are now under the umbrella of my potential to earn.

Once again, the boundaries in my life have become less rigid. As an entrepreneur, the separation between my work income and my personal income is gone. Prior to becoming an entrepreneur, I had my job and its related cash flow, and I also had real estate and personal investments. Now all of this is in one place. It's O.K. now for me to spend time on my rentals during the day because it's all under the umbrella of my life. Rethinking these assets (if you have them) may free up a source of funding to begin or advance your venture.

KEY POINTS:

As you start or grow your own business and attempt to define a more ideal life, obstacles will present themselves constantly. View each obstacle as an opportunity to rethink your problem. If the "solution" you want is not readily or easily available, maybe it's not the best solution for you. Life has a way of sending us messages, and it's our job to pay attention. Obstacles can be amazing opportunities to think beyond obvious solutions to alternatives that are better, faster, and cheaper!

EXERCISES:

- What barriers do you see today that will keep you from starting/advancing your own business?
- How can you restate each of these to open yourself up to unique solutions? (Look to why you need/want each of the things that are barriers.)
- After redefining the problem from what you want to why you need these things, what unique solutions can you present?

How often—even before we began—have we declared a task "impossible"?

And how often have we construed a picture of ourselves as being inadequate? ...a great deal depends upon the thought patterns we choose and on the persistence with which we affirm them.

—Piero Ferrucci

Chapter 8

Poet and Warrior

*Coming to terms with a redefined you: balancing
the corporate warrior with your spiritual self*

As written earlier, Confucius said that we are each
capable of being "both poet and warrior." What a liberating
idea this is! Many of us see ourselves as somewhere between
an Armani-wearing investment banker and someone selling
smoothies on the beach in Florida. We are pressured to be
consistent, and consistency is everything in Western society.
Presidencies have been lost due to the perception that they
were inconsistent. As entrepreneurs or potential entrepreneurs, we have one foot firmly embedded in the known (in
our job, in our paycheck, in the list of things that are expected
of us and help us feel important and secure) and the other foot
in the unknown (where we yearn for freedom and want to get
back to childhood playfulness and lose the list and the items
to be complete by next quarter). We know that we are partly
defined by the culture of the company we work for and even
more specifically by the position we hold there.

But we also know the part of ourselves that is defined
neither by our industry, company, or position or even by our
family and friends. As we think about making a major life
shift by considering a more entrepreneurial opportunity, we
are bound to hear a number of things: "This isn't like you"
or "I don't know where you fit—you're neither this nor that."

Several years ago, a friend said, "Dietmeyer, you're an

enigma." This made me uncomfortable as I struggled to determine what "camp" I fit into. I looked for a definition that placed me in a channel where I felt comfortable. For years I felt out of place everywhere, fit nowhere. I rode Harleys on the weekends with my biker buddies and went to big corporate events in my blue suit and white shirt: neither felt right, even though I enjoyed aspects of both. I struggled to find a more definitive slot to plug myself into.

After many years pondering this, I realized that the middle ground was my niche. I am neither this nor that, but am all those things! I like aspects of the corporate environment, but I also admire struggling entrepreneurs. Here are a couple of bottom lines:

Either the poet or the warrior is stronger, even though they're both present in you. You do not have to become one or the other.

I am comfortable almost anywhere. I fit almost anywhere. I am both a poet and a warrior. I am deathly serious about the quality of my work and the impact I have on my client organizations. I want my firm to be consistent, tight, and professional. I wrench on my own Harley, decorate my own home, and have rediscovered many objects, toys, and activities from my youth that were abandoned because they seemed inappropriate to my corporate image. As the part of you that has been repressed begins to assert itself, you will either begin to feel the struggle between the poet and the warrior in you, or those around you will say things like, "That's not like you." Some may even go so far as to say, "We're afraid for you and think there might be something wrong."

My theory is that most people value consistency in others because they are most comfortable when their own lives are well-defined and fit within certain predetermined boundaries. When some people perceive us changing, they are compelled to redraw their own lines. It's tough enough to deal with our own internal struggle—we also can look forward to others asking us the same questions.

Many years ago, I was sitting in the Fountain Court Restaurant at the Biltmore Hotel in Santa Barbara, California. This was the place to be seen. Jonathan Winters, Julia Child, and John Travolta dined there regularly. I was Director of Sales at the Biltmore and was entertaining two vice presidents from a bicycle-manufacturing concern. All of a sudden I felt as if everyone in the restaurant was staring at me (they weren't), that I was the only person who didn't belong there (I wasn't). I was certain they all knew I was the son of a bartender and a Polish housekeeper, that immediately after high school, I had driven a dump truck and labored on construction sites, that I had only a high-school diploma and two or three community-college courses under my belt. Who was I kidding with this Biltmore gig? I was completely miscast and out of my element.

In fact, I belonged there as much as anyone else. I was way ahead of the curve at that point in my life, but it was the right place for me to be at the time, regardless of how I or other people viewed me. It wasn't until I quit attempting to be a Santa Barbara blueblood that I actually began to fit in. In fact, milking the poor-blue-collar-kid-done-good thing proved to be a useful platform for me! Even so, the stories of my upbringing began to take on some poetic license.

This same thing occurred when I began to present myself as the senior partner and managing director of my own firm. It's called the impostor complex, and it's bound to happen as you redefine yourself. King George (in The King's Speech) felt he didn't deserve to be King of England. It's estimated that 70% of high achievers feel like impostors, certain their present level of achievement does not result from true ability and others will soon discover the frauds they really are. The impostor complex is common in major life changes—all that has defined you is challenged as you shed your skin and new parts of you emerge. Many of us stay with "good" because "great" requires us to face tough elements of change like the impostor complex. Of all my memories of Santa Barbara, this is one of the most significant, yet at the time I wanted to escape in the worst possible way! Yet the only way to slowly shed the skin of being raised blue collar in the South Side of Chicago was to push the envelope, face the demons. It was not in spite of but because of how I grew up that I ended up where I was.

The same holds true for you. Don't apologize for being the daughter of a laborer or a Harvard MBA. Go with what you are. Build on who you really are and where you really came from and, most importantly, where you want to be with your life. It's O.K. to be both poet and warrior.

You know right now which one is stronger—the poet or the warrior—and you know right now which one is being under nurtured. Pay attention to them. Nurture them. Define yourself by what's important to you and be ready for the onslaught of concern and criticism as you redefine your relationships with those around you. So many times the question of "balance" came up for me. Just remember that the balance you search for may be seen as inconsistency by others who prefer a more specific role in life and more defined boundaries. The poet and the warrior, for me, are clear now. The question for you is: how can your epitaph show you how to begin accomplishing your life today in all that you do? Take the time to find the aspects of your life that are truly you and the aspects that are missing.

Every child is an artist. The challenge is how to remain an artist once he grows up.

—Pablo Picasso

As a child, I was fascinated with motors: motorcycles, hot rods, boats. I grew up with grease on my hands. I also grew up water-skiing and dirt-biking. None of these things had been a part of my life for 20 years. Several years ago, I bought an old Harley. Early last summer, I purchased an old ski boat and a 1955 Chevy truck, which I now drive as my primary transportation. The Harley garnered the first mid-life crisis comments, the boat provoked more, and the old truck finally convinced people that I was crazy.

In fact, I was crazy many years before to eliminate so many of the simple pleasures that had defined my life. My life had been slowly circumscribed by what was expected of me. I had begun to redefine my life—and, in the words of my assistant, Ann Cale, "People don't change, they become who they are." (If they're lucky, I would add.)

Desiderata suggests that we "take kindly the counsel of years gracefully surrendering the things of youth." I used to think this meant that in order to grow up we had to stop enjoying the pleasures of our childhoods. Now I interpret it to mean that some things do fade, but there's no reason to rid yourself of the pleasures and pastimes that are part of who you are simply because you think you "should."

After making "the break," you may sense a power loss. Breathe for a moment; take stock. Enjoy the "middle ground" between what defined you and your own new definition. You will find different parts of your personality emerging, and some may seem contradictory or at odds. Remember that you can be "both poet and warrior."

A loss of power can be a good thing. It can help you strip away what defines you and truly focus on what is underneath your title, money, and job description. Don't rush to redefine your new life with trappings of the past that simply replace what you consciously left behind. This middle ground may be uncomfortable, but it also gives you a prime opportunity to rediscover what is within you trying to get out.

I heard this stage defined by a futurist as an attempt to lower the water level in a river. When we begin to lower the water, we will see some rocks. Instead of objectively observing them and learning about them, our first impulse is to dump the water back in and cover them up again!

Whether you're a new entrepreneur or considering becoming one, this opportunity to find balance, to draw off some aspects of your personal and professional life, is priceless. Remember, when someone says, "Well, that's not like you," it may serve to let them know that you are, in fact, more like yourself than you've ever been! As I write this, I am in Santa Barbara, California. I am neither on vacation nor working—I am just here being me in my custom-designed life. While here, I spent time with a friend who left a corporate career many years ago. The life she has now is radically different from her past, and is clearly defined for her and her family based on what they want versus the accepted norm. She mentioned that, as she looks back over her many corporate relocations and promotions, she sees them as being "out of sync" with where she wanted to be, but many of the opportunities afforded her seemed "too good to pass up." In retrospect, she can see that they really weren't too good to pass up, based on where she really wanted to be.

KEY POINTS:

Many of us have parts of our personalities that have been put away in storage. Part of redefining success in your own life (by taking control of your destiny through an entrepreneurial venture) is to identify and nurture these forgotten or neglected parts of ourselves. Be prepared for discomfort—in yourself and in those around you—as you redefine and remember who you are. As you begin living a life more appropriate for you, stay focused on your target, on what you really want in your life as the new momentum picks up.

We must attend very carefully to childhood to catch early glimpses of the daimon in action, to grasp its intentions and not block its way.

—James Hillman, The Soul's Code

Chapter 9

Success is Meeting With Triumph and Disaster and Treating Both Impostors the Same

Maintaining an even keel by being process- versus event-focused

> *Success is meeting with triumph and disaster and treating both impostors the same.*
>
> —Rudyard Kipling

This quote should probably be inscribed on every entrepreneur's badge (if we were required to carry one). As an entrepreneur, you'll need to learn how to reframe the way you see positive events as well as obstacles in your path. The high you feel when a potential investor professes interest in your business and the devastating low of losing your first big client are equally exhausting and can be equally dangerous to your health.

A friend is a brilliant engineer who developed a technology that purifies common tap water. Three years before, my friend had happened upon a water store franchise and thought, "Well, this is interesting—perhaps I'll put together an investment group to open a series of these stores across the Midwest." As he approached investors, he realized that most investors wanted to be franchisors, not franchisees. When he looked closely at the business, he realized that the only things detracting from profits were rent and people to staff the store.

Given these two challenges, he set out to determine how

he could not only be a franchisor, but also increase the profit margins in the business. He realized that he would have to develop his own technology in the form of a water-purification system, so off he went. In cooperation with a Swiss firm, he developed a system that acted like a small purification plant. His strategy was to install these units in multiple-use buildings, buildings with residences, restaurants, and businesses (like the John Hancock in Chicago). He figured the demand from all three sources would be enough to keep the system busy, since the quality of tap water in most major cities is becoming dangerously low.

At that point in the business, my friend had his savings, his wife's savings, and investment capital from most of their family members on the line. One day, he calmly mentioned that he had run into a "slightly difficult" situation. It seems the city of Chicago had a 100-year-old law on the books prohibiting the resale of Chicago water.

I was surprised by his composure: his supply of raw material was being cut off! He had asked me to invest in the business, and I began to regret my investment. It seemed unlikely that a 100-year-old law would be overturned, but he remained calm in the middle of what I saw as a major setback.

My friend got the law changed. In fact, he decided on a entirely different strategy for his business: putting his systems into the larger health-oriented grocery chains. Today he is the top seller of bottled water in the south. His brand, H2Only, has taken off like a rocket, he recently won third place at an international bottled-water convention. His initial roadblocks forced him to rethink and rethink his strategy until most of the kinks were worked out. Roadblocks that seemed insurmountable actually caused him to redefine the business before he made large capital investments in the wrong areas.

Sometime our tendency to "make something happen" overrides the natural process. If something goes wrong, we simply accept it, missing out on a helpful message about the need to adjust our course. If something positive is happening and begins to slip away, we pursue it with dogged determination, when it may be wiser to let it go.

Almost immediately after leaving my corporate job, my new company received a lead from a major insurance company that wanted a contract in excess of $200,000. This was our first client. I had projected that if we were extremely successful in the first year, we might generate $100,000 with 8–10 clients. Here the company was, two weeks old, and we had a very solid lead on a Fortune 100 client. If this kept up, we could easily have a $700,000–$900,000 first year. I had made the right decision: I couldn't believe how easy it was, and I berated myself for not leaving corporate life sooner.

About six weeks later, I had the opportunity to address the regional chapter of a national association at a monthly luncheon that was full of potential customers. Such an ideal opportunity right out of the chute—my fledgling firm was going to get a chance to strut its stuff in front of 50–60 brand-name companies. I built my presentation with all the careful planning I had learned in many years of presenting at senior management meetings as well as at industry association and company sales meetings. I was very confident in my public-speaking ability and was not only prepared for but electrified by this wonderful opportunity.

We were nearing closure with our "big fish" of six weeks before, and we couldn't believe our luck that this client was going to be able to attend the presentation as our guest. What an awesome opportunity—this client would see me as the keynote speaker at a very prestigious association luncheon filled with management from major companies!

I was introduced and began my interactive presentation. About 10 minutes into the presentation, a very direct (almost hostile) participant "went for me" verbally. The group wasn't reacting positively, as most groups had in the past—in fact, they looked bored stiff and were staring at me like I wasn't even speaking English. I muddled through the next 30 minutes—I've never wanted to get off a stage more quickly in my entire life.

The written evaluations of my presentation confirmed my suspicions: I had created an equity withdrawal in the brand name of my company. I went home and read through each evaluation. One was especially painful: "What was his point?" Not exactly the type of thing to build confidence in the cutting-edge nature of my new firm. I ended up that Friday afternoon in bed, in the fetal position, in my boxers—not exactly a captain of industry!

Recall that in the audience was the invited guest, a huge potential client. This major insurance company had the potential of purchasing more than $200,000 in services from our firm.

On Monday morning, I called my contact at the insurance company to apologize: all the help he had been giving us was for naught—I had blown the deal. "Funny," he said, "I have an e-mail from my boss, who attended your presentation. It says: 'Saw Brian at the Marriott on Friday, liked the structure of his presentation. I would be proud to have him on stage for us.'" My contact paused, then added, "Oh ye of little faith!" Later on that year, I was asked to facilitate a session at the same association's annual conference.

Eastern philosophy teaches us that things are neither good or bad, they just are what's happening right now. As a new entrepreneur with a fragile sense of stability, you may tend to see events in isolation. (If this happens today it will be good, or if that happens tomorrow it will be bad.) In reality, it's about process, a chain of events that lead to places we never thought we'd go. Over time, many events tend to play out into a full story, and with hindsight we can see that events are what they are and everything contributes to the outcome. Events do not simply fit into categories of "good" and "bad" as they relate to our perceptions. Your ability to remain cautiously optimistic when you close a big deal instead of being absolutely ecstatic and your ability to stay positive, rational, and focused when you lose a big deal are both essential to enjoying the entrepreneurial life. In the face of adversity, confidence is key; in the face of success, a humble nature will serve you well.

I don't mean to imply that you have to become a Vulcan (like Spock), but rather that you should enjoy the process of defining your new life. When your business is very successful, it will be bigger and more complex than you ever imagined. You'll yearn for the early days and wish you'd been a more rational observer of the process and your reaction to specific events. Redefining yourself as an entrepreneur offers incredible opportunities to study yourself in key situations and redefine how you feel, what you think, and how you react to and process new stimuli. Isn't this, after all, the underlying reason why you want to consider "being out on your own?"

When you talk about your new idea or venture, most people will ask about products, markets, pricing, and financial risk. On the other hand, if you mention your new opportunity to those who have been there, they'll probably ask you about your "redefinition of self."

I have a friend who was head of the American Marketing Association. When I first told him that I had started my own business, he was the first one to ask, "How does it feel to reinvent yourself?" That question got my attention. I was mostly focusing on the business plan, but he made it apparent that there was so much more to this process by focusing on the human element, on the "why" of the "what." The business is what we are doing, our personal growth is why most of us do it. Why is much more interesting and fulfilling. Why is the opportunity for personal growth.

A postscript to the presentation drama: in all my years at a big company, I had either presented at industry functions where my firm carried a lot of weight as a $14-billion company, at customer functions where we were wining and dining clients at our expense, or executing sales training meetings with my sales team, who saw these meetings as political opportunities. In my corporate life, when I walked into a room to present, I had the horsepower of a vice-president job at a $14-billion Fortune 100 firm. When I went out on my own, I had lost everything that gave me credibility before I ever opened my mouth. Those things got me in the door, but the evaluation of who I was and what I could do was zero-based. I was stripped of the armor that had protected me. I was as prepared as I typically needed to be in my old world, but the entrepreneurial world taught me a quick and elegant lesson: what worked as an employee does not work as an owner. Small organizations are out there doing brilliant things—and the market expects nothing less than brilliance. My preparation time from now on will have to be tripled, and so will yours.

Probably the most important things I've learned after leaving a company are the almost brutal directness of the market in its valuation of our work, and the outrageous quality of work coming from my competitors. Small firms are relentless in pursuit of quality and customer care. On the other hand, our clients fully expect to have their expectations exceeded in every aspect of our work, from sales to delivery to follow-up, including the ongoing relationship. The benefit of the huge, throbbing mass of distribution and worldwide brand names no longer benefit you. It's all about the work (finally!).

Early on I lost a big (overnight services) client to a competitor. It seemed like a bad thing at the time. But now, as I reflect on the process of our business, it wasn't necessarily bad. Two things would have happened with this new account. First, we would not have been prepared for the onslaught of activity related to taking on two new accounts at once. Second, our products and processes are better today because we grew at a slow, gradual pace and had time to reinvest and refine what we do. If we had received that contract, we probably would have underperformed in the customer's eyes by delivering a premature product and subsequently lost the opportunity to slowly grow and reinvest in our product.

For me, country music has always been a great source of street-level philosophy. One line from a song by Garth Brooks could be the anthem for entrepreneurs: "Some of God's greatest gifts are unanswered prayers." Enjoy the process instead of reflexively evaluating events. Challenge yourself to go back 5, 10, 15, 20 years and think about events that led to events that led to other events. You'll see that painful events often led you to a better place in the long run. Likewise, consider things that seemed to be answers to prayers at the time but didn't turn out well. (Think about the long-term happiness of most lottery winners.)

KEY POINTS:

You'll find your entrepreneurial life much more fulfilling if you can objectively greet each situation that comes your way and take it for what it is. It is neither good nor bad, it simply is what it is. It also helps immensely to think about each event in terms of how it fits into the larger scheme of things. Let the scenario play itself out over time—sometimes months or years later, you'll become aware that things weren't at all what they seemed in the beginning.

Chapter 10

Sure, It's Easy for You...
I Didn't Sleep Last Night!

Stress management for your new life

One of our early clients was a major pharmaceutical company. Before our first meeting with them, we spent months customizing almost 80% of our base product to speak to their needs. We had "design team" conference calls and went well out of our way to exceed their expectations and deliver the equivalent of a custom-made suit. We spent about four times as much in terms of resources as we had anticipated. We wanted to so far exceed this customer's expectations that we didn't even bill for most of these changes. As we neared the first program, we could hardly wait to deliver the product and "blow the client away."

About three hours into the first day of the meeting, one of the participants came up to me and said, "This is a great program for managed-care executives. It was obviously written for this position." I beamed. Then he added, "I wish I were one." "Explain," I said. He did: "I am a division manager. That's radically different from the managed-care executive role." "Hmmmm," I said, "this must be tough on you." "It's tough on most of us," he said, "since 28 of the 30 persons in the room are division managers."

Panic set in: I was fighting a brilliant battle on the wrong battlefield. We found out that the target audience was called away to a last-minute meeting and they back-filled our event with a different group. That evening we went back and rewrote the program as much as possible for the second day. When it was all said and done, the program was below average and the client evaluations were tough. One said, "Who was this guy? We have one of them at every meeting."

This was the first event for our second client. It was only about 25% of our contracted work with them and I feared the worst: the other 75% would be at risk. I was frozen for days. My initial feedback from the client was cool at best; not bad, but distant. For the next week, I could barely bring myself to work or even sleep. Running the tape over and over again in my brain, I realized it wasn't my fault, but I also knew that the consultant (me) would take the hit, not internal management.

After being in a comatose state for the first week, I came back to my office the following Monday and began to work. Slowly, I realized that with effective and efficient activity came stress relief. The more I worked at redefining our second client meeting and learning from our mistakes, the lower my stress level became. Zen philosophy often refers to the "second arrow". The idea being that we get hit with the first arrow and there is real pain there, then we feel bad about that, why me, why did I get shot, anger at the person who shot me… all are 2nd, 3rd and 4th arrows that we could choose to avoid. Or in the words of my father, a not so famous philosopher, "son, that will bother you just about as long as you allow it." The pain is real, don't dwell, don't get angry, stay away from woe is me… do something about it.

Here's the point: action relieves stress. Not just any healthy action, but action designed to lower stress. If you have pain in your knee, you can find some sort of physical therapy that will help, or you can just lay around and wallow in your pain. Every single time things get really tough in the entrepreneurial trenches, you can relieve your stress through positive action. Do something about the problem. If you have no sales, go find customers. If your product has a deficiency, fix it. If your skills are below par in an area important to your success, go get the skills.

We had an entry-level sales representative who was having a tough time due to the long sales cycle in our business. Success just wasn't coming fast enough, and he began to stress. Stress kept him from sleeping at night. He tried to relieve the lack of sleep with some efficient drinking, but he still couldn't sleep and the spiral began. He started coming in late, then missing work. I finally said, "Let's talk about this." He explained his problems with stressing over no sales, and I said, "So, go get some more customers." He replied, "You don't understand—I can't even sleep at night. This is not an easy position I'm in." I told him he was right; I slept beautifully at night: 7–8 hours without interruption. "See?" he said, "it's easier for you."

We then discussed the fact that his stress was my stress—in fact, his low sales performance was a double-whammy for me. I had put less emphasis on sales since he arrived by giving the sales function over to him, and I was also paying his salary—therefore, I had the right to be almost twice as sleep-deprived! But to what end?

Stress detracts from positive activity. Stress makes us consider deals we might not otherwise consider. Stress makes us lose sleep, become irritable, and lowers our probability of success. Stress takes all the fun out of running your business. Whether or not you stress out, the fundamental issue that served to justify your stress is still there. So, given your choices, would you choose to face tough issues fresh, with a good night's sleep—or tired, with a hangover?

Look at your stress rationally. You're choosing to make a tough situation worse. This is masochistic behavior. Why are you "choosing" to let the environmental factors of your business impact your attitude? Worrying has a huge impact on your business and your life, and it's almost always harmful. All you can do is to find activities that help relieve the cause of your pain. Do it with a smile on your face, because these events will impact you over and over again. Over time, stress will kill you. Pay great attention to crucial situations in your business and take strong and positive action to correct them. Then relax and enjoy the challenge.

I remember hearing stories about general contractors who financed the building of their first speculative home on six credit cards, each maxed out at $25,000 each. They slept in sleeping bags in the unfurnished home, hiding from creditors until the closing was completed and funding was executed. At that point, they paid off the credit cards and were rewarded for their risk by their profits. More importantly, they were now in possession of a wealth of stories and memories of their first project. These stories will penetrate the fabric of who they are over the next 25 years, and the profits from their 200th home will not be nearly as rewarding as the first. So why not know that now and enjoy the process? If you're feeling stressed, do something that begins to lower your stress.

At one point early in my entrepreneurship, I was checking out of a beautiful resort in the West Indies where I had been doing work for a client in Barbados (good work if you can get it). There was a problem, and my first credit card was denied, then my second, and then my third. Mind you, I had never had a credit balance anywhere but a mortgage. I had no car payment, no credit card debt, nothing. I hate having debt and here I was maxed out and late on three credit cards. I was embarrassed, stressed, and ready to crawl under the hotel front desk. Instead, I asked for the phone and explained slowly and politely to the AMEX agent that I was in a foreign country, had all of $20 in my pocket, and not only needed them to pay my hotel bill but advance me some cash.

Through gentle persuasion, they did it. I knew that with some pending receivables coming in, all would be paid up; I was merely caught in what is commonly referred to as a cash-flow crunch. Once the agent had agreed to pay the bill and advance some cash, I walked away from the desk clerk (who looked at me like I was some sort of quick-change artist), and climbed into a taxi with a smile from ear to ear, realizing that I was becoming the sort of edge-of-the-envelope entrepreneur I had always admired.

This situation stressed me out for about 2.5 seconds, until I realized that stress would play a big role in the quality of my life for the next couple of hours. At that point I began to enjoy the process and revel in the realities of life without the corporate safety net. I was still stuck in a foreign country with no cash in an embarrassing situation—I merely took action to eliminate the stress and to have fun with it. This story is much more memorable and brings more smiles to my face than all the times I checked out of hotels and the credit card worked!

Potential clients who seem promising fall flat, and calls made to non-receptive parties generate business. Many things that happen in the early phases of your business might seem to be back-breaking or year-making, but more often than not they are neither.

KEY POINTS:

Choosing to lie awake (stressing) about a business problem serves no positive purpose. In fact, it is debilitating to your emotional and physical health. Each time you stress out, choose to change your attitude about it, have fun with it, and realize that these are the challenges you've asked for as an entrepreneur. Use each situation to test who you are. After an attitude switch, do something constructive to get rid of the pain. Remember that well-placed action reduces stress.

Chapter 11

Loving Kindness

Drives profit, builds brand equity

My VP Sales and I were going to see the President of a $4b Atlanta based company. He was willing to see us but had been quite testy during the process leading up to our appointment. We stopped in the local Starbucks to get coffee before our appointment and asked the cashier to tell us if the company we were going to see was close by. She said, "It's right up there and their President comes in here nearly every day." "Oh really," we say. "What is he like?" She hesitates and then conspiratorially says, "...a dick, a real dick. He has a huge attitude and makes us custom make everything!"

We walked out to the car and my VP said, "Crap... this is gonna be tough." We stopped and talked about it—who is this guy, what are his challenges, what is he afraid of, etc. Not his business problems—we knew all about their software, how they evolved over time, how they were shifting to cloud computing, competitors, etc. What we focused on was him, the human, what was on his mind. This was a privately held firm and the President was fourth generation family. He probably grew up living, breathing, eating, sleeping, being part of a fully merged family and company where all was intertwined. He had all that pressure to keep the family business moving, way more stress than simply running a nameless, faceless corporation. Not only that, we assumed that somewhere down deep he always wondered if he could have made it on his own, without all the good decisions and groundwork of his ancestors. It was fear beneath that anger and attitude we reckoned. Wow, our attitude changed and we thought that we were going into this meeting with love, pure love for this guy and his struggles. I swear, we did this. We walked into the room and he was what we thought, right from the get go. We didn't respond with fear, we didn't respond with ego, we responded and were coming from pure love. It took maybe 15 minutes before he was joking, and even further, his team of leaders began changing as well—the entire tone of the meeting changed. This wasn't a ruse, it wasn't a scam to get business, we really cared for this guy.

In his book, *The Wise Heart*, Jack Kornfield points out that eastern philosophy has documented this phenomenon of "mood contagion" or limbic resonance. If a person filled with panic walks into a room, we feel it immediately. When a joyful person walks in, we can feel that state as well.

> *When we see the goodness of those before us, the dignity in them resonates with our admiration and respect.*
>
> —Jack Kornfield

Italian scientist, Giacomo Rizzolatti, discovered a class of brain cells called mirror neurons. Through these neurons we actually feel the emotions and intentions of others. I have a friend who runs a small, wildly successful financial consulting firm. I once asked her what it was that made her so successful. I was expecting to hear about her powerful intellectual property, or the experience of her years on Wall Street, or her finance degrees. But what she said was, "I love my clients." "Right," I said. "I love mine too but..." "No really," she says. "Let's say I am running a finance workshop for non-financial managers. I have 20 people in the room—I want every single person to be comfortable, I want them to walk out supremely confident in their financial skills, I do not want anyone fearing of embarrassment or being called out, etc." She had used pure caring and love for the sake of caring and love to be the best of the best. This lesson has come so many times in so many ways. Before I did my first speech, I was very nervous and wondering all about how people would receive me. My friend Bob told me, "It's not about you, it's about them. Focus on them, on helping them, on caring for them."

Kindness and compassion are among the principal things that make our lives meaningful. They are a source of everlasting happiness and joy. They are the foundation of a good heart, the heart of one that acts out of a desire to help others. Through kindness toward everyone else we ensure our own benefit. This is a matter of common sense. Consideration for others is worthwhile because our happiness is inextricably bound up with the happiness of others.

—The Dalai Lama, preface of Piero Ferucci's
The Power of Kindness

At my company meeting last year, the theme was "The Power of Kindness." The idea being that the most ruthless business strategy there is, is one where we truly care more for the people we work for—our clients. If our caring came from love for wanting to help those individuals reach whatever their personal goals were by making them professionally successful.

We used many of the themes from the book of the same name by Piero Ferucci:
• Loyalty
• Compassion
• Empathy
• Patience

- Trust
- Respect
- Service
- Flexibility

All of these are the most powerful business strategies known to man and they also happen to be drivers of loving kindness.

Ferucci writes mostly about kindness on a "retail level," person to person. He does, however, offer the following:

> *And what about business and commerce? Here again we reach the same conclusions. Firms that exploit their workers, deceive the customer, and create a waste culture, will perhaps gain the in the short term, but in the long run they compete less favorable than those who that, in their own interests, do not take advantage of employees, respect the environment, and place themselves at the service of clients.*
>
> —Piero Ferrucci, The Power of Kindness

My mom was a waitress and when I was about 15 she came home with a $100 tip on a $100 meal. This kind of thing was commonplace for her and I finally asked her why it was that she made so much money and if she was tired of waiting on people (she was a housekeeper and waitress). She looked blown away. She looked me square in the eyes and described serving others with the sort of nobility one has for saving lives.

"You don't understand," she told me. "You never know what is happening at that table when you walk up to it—they could have just met, first date, on the verge of divorce, just had a death in the family, maybe a struggling young family for their first time out in a year! Do you understand the impact that this dinner might have on events going forward?"

This is love. This is human caring. This is good business and also allows us to sleep well at night. I tell my wife the same thing before she goes on stage with her band, "You never know the importance of positively impacting the audience night. Don't worry about how technically savvy you might be in your music, focus on sending love to the audience and loving to perform for them... the rest will take care of itself."

The notion that art and science don't mix and that business is soulless is crazy. When I met my wife, who is an artist, many of her friends were artists and were concerned that she had "sold out" by getting married to a "business man." This was hysterical to me, I had never thought of the world in these terms, but evidently, artists are somehow on a higher spiritual and righteous path than heathen business people.

After being shocked, I pointed out to her that I had used my business skills to manage bands as a volunteer business manager and produced theatre in a nonprofit. I also asked her who it was that was on the guest list for her shows (other artists) and who it was that was in the audience paying (all my business pals). My rant went somewhat further to ask her who sat on the boards of theatre companies we were involved with—artists or business people.

The world, as I see it, is full of poet warriors, neither this nor that, the middle way as it were. It's time to allow ourselves to define ourselves based on a more balanced view, and less pre-defined, made up guidelines. As we've spent years together my wife has met many of the people I am so fortunate to be surrounded by... Poet Warriors.

Loving compassion also helps you decide when to "cut bait" and make the right decisions. One of our most successful consultants drove huge amounts of revenue to the firm and our clients worshipped him. At the same time, we didn't trust him and felt that he brought too much negativity and bad energy internally to the company. We have this company motto that we are a firm that is run by "smart people who are good people." This particular consultant was off the charts on the "smart people" side. For years I was not sure people believed we really invested in that motto as we allowed the "good people" side to slip due to our fear of losing out on big revenue streams. It was love and compassion and the desire to do well by everyone, including my internal associates, that made it quite easy to cut the cord with this consultant.

A lot of people will say, "Sure, this sounds all nice but the reality is that all the bad asses make it to the top in my organization by being ruthless." Please, don't forget that operating with loving kindness, if it comes genuinely from the heart, will win every time. There is no more "ruthless" competition than caring more than everyone else and as I have pointed out, it's also one that allows you to sleep well at night. One thing I know for sure, having spent almost 20 years in a Fortune 100 company, is that "the truth will out." The nice, quiet, super bright, caring person in the corner will get prompted; the one stepping on everyone to get what they want will take a fall. It takes a while in bureaucracies but it will happen.

Business is not separate from life, it is life. And when we think of them as separate and do things out of sync with who we wish to be, we tear at our soul.

I want to close with a paradigm shift. I love Michael Moore and he has done plenty of good with his life. There is plenty of bad news about corporations for plenty of good reasons. In his movie, *Capitalism: A Love Story*, he very powerfully and accurately points them out.

I would also like to see him make a documentary that is forward looking—one that focuses on the emerging trend of social corporate consciousness. You and I both know lots of people today that are doing this in their own small businesses. We also have some great corporate icons leading the way.

Making money is the best art.

—Andy Warhol

Richard Branson of Virgin Group is one of top 5 richest people in the United Kingdom. His ventures include gaming, mobile, music, and airlines. He also runs Virgin Unite, a nonprofit foundation of Virgin Group. 100% of overhead is covered by RB and he works with people like Peter Gabriel and Nelson Mandela. The goal of Virgin Unite is:

To create positive and lasting change and ensure that business truly is a force for good.

Further they add:

We unite people to tackle tough social and environmental problems with an entrepreneurial approach. Our aim is to help revolutionize the way businesses and the social sector work together—driving business as a force for good. This is based on the belief that this is the only way we can address the scale and urgency of the challenges facing the world today. Virgin Unite also works on behalf of vulnerable young people across the globe.

O.K., we all know who Bill Gates of Microsoft fame is, right? One of the richest men in the world. But do we know about all the good work done by him and his wife as part of his foundation?

The Bill and Melinda Gates Foundation is guided by the belief that every life has equal value and works to help people lead healthy, productive lives. In developing countries, it focuses on improving people's health and giving them the

83

chance to lift themselves out of hunger and extreme poverty. In the United States, it seeks to ensure that all people—especially those with the fewest resources—have access to the opportunities they need to succeed in school and life.

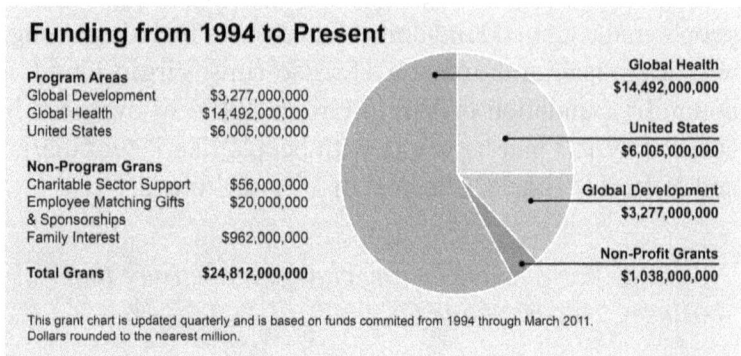

Funding from 1994 to Present

Program Areas	
Global Development	$3,277,000,000
Global Health	$14,492,000,000
United States	$6,005,000,000
Non-Program Grans	
Charitable Sector Support	$56,000,000
Employee Matching Gifts & Sponsorships	$20,000,000
Family Interest	$962,000,000
Total Grans	**$24,812,000,000**

Global Health
$14,492,000,000

United States
$6,005,000,000

Global Development
$3,277,000,000

Non-Profit Grants
$1,038,000,000

This grant chart is updated quarterly and is based on funds commited from 1994 through March 2011. Dollars rounded to the nearest million.

A quote from Gates:

The world's poorest will not be visiting government leaders to make their case, unlike other constituencies, so I want to help make their case by describing the progress and the potential I see in key areas of health and development. Perhaps it is ironic for someone who has been so lucky to talk about the needs of those who have not.

I believe it is in the rich world's enlightened self-interest to continue investing in foreign aid. If societies can't provide for people's basic health, if they can't feed and educate people, then their populations and problems will grow and the world will be a less stable place.

Whether you believe it a moral imperative or in the rich world's enlightened self-interest, securing the conditions that will lead to a healthy, prosperous future for everyone is a goal I believe we all share.

Peter Gabriel is a British singer, musician, and song-writer who rose to fame as the lead vocalist and flautist of the progressive rock group Genesis. After leaving Genesis, Gabriel went on to a successful solo career. More recently he has focused on producing and promoting world music and pioneering digital distribution methods for music. He has also been involved in various humanitarian efforts.

In 1986 he started what has become a longstanding association with Amnesty International, becoming a pioneering participant in all 28 of Amnesty's Human Rights Concerts—a series of music events and tours staged by the U.S. Section of Amnesty International between 1986–1998. He performed during the six-concert U.S. tour, A Conspiracy of Hope, in June 1986; the twenty-concert Human Rights Now! world tour in 1988; the Chile: Embrace of Hope Concert in 1990 and at The Paris Concert For Amnesty International in 1998. He also performed in Amnesty's Secret Policeman's Ball benefit shows. He spoke of his support for Amnesty on NBC's *Today Show* in 1986.

Inspired by the social activism he encountered in his work with Amnesty, in 1992 Gabriel co-founded WITNESS, a nonprofit group that equips, trains, and supports locally-based organizations worldwide to use video and the Internet in human rights documentation and advocacy. My wife and I have been fortunate enough to attend their annual fundraiser, the work they do is astounding and awe inspiring.

On 18 July 2007, in Johannesburg, South Africa, Nelson Mandela announced the formation of a new group, Global Elders, in a speech he delivered on the occasion of his 89th birthday. The present members of this group are Desmond Tutu, Graça Machel, Kofi Annan, Ela Bhatt, Lakhdar Brahimi, Gro Harlem Brundtland, Fernando Henrique Cardoso, Jimmy Carter, Mary Robinson, Muhammad Yunus, and Aung San Suu Kyi (with an empty chair for her).

The Elders will be independently funded by a group of

"Founders," including Branson and Gabriel.

There is a strong undercurrent and a rising prominence of bringing art and science, poet and warrior, loving kindness and business closer together. It is incumbent upon us as entrepreneurs to foster this growth.

Chapter 12

Tie It All Together

A review and connection of chapters 1–11

Thinking About It

One of the most important parts of starting is to allow yourself time to "detox" and go through the uncomfortable shedding of all your adopted success measurements. Your own personal measurements will come to you quickly enough—resist the temptation to recreate or run back to what you know.

When you think about starting your entrepreneurial firm, life tests your resolve and gives you the skills you need by presenting a series of obstacles. The first obstacle is finding a way to give yourself permission to pursue your goals. You need to move beyond negative internal messages (such as "This is not rational," "It's immature," and so on) and realize that these are merely early barriers and tests.

When you're considering this change, it is an ideal time to challenge where your existing success measurements come from. Writing your zero-based epitaph should help you quiet the noise that has influenced what you see as success. Focusing not on what your epitaph will be, but what you want it to be will truly drive short-term success measurements in your life. Short-term success measurements are the tactics and your epitaph is your strategy. Tactics are so much easier to decide on and execute with a clear strategy, direction, or endpoint in mind.

After you think about this change, you need to begin the process of executing your idea. The first few steps are scary. What do you do? Here it's important to remember that you know what to do better than anyone—it's your idea. Realize that you do know how. Positive thinking about and a clear, visual perspective on where you are going are powerful tools. The clearer and more detailed your thoughts and visualizations, the better. You also need to remember that how you think impacts what you do and what you get. You will attract this vision of a new and positive future, but you will also attract your greatest fears. If you really feel it will happen, it will!

In addition to a clear vision, you need an objective audit of your "technical skills." You know what your strengths are, but it's more important to clearly identify your weaknesses as they relate to your new role. Your existing strengths and weaknesses may not transfer to a more entrepreneurial role. Take a close look at key success factors and skills in your new role and identify your strong and weak points relative to them. When you find a technical shortcoming for your new venture, you need to find a way to learn it yourself or find someone who can support you in this key success area.

After developing a clear vision and identifying potential barriers, it's time to act. But remember: lots of activity does not equal good activity. You need to act in ways that are purposeful and that lead to your vision.

Finally, remember that sitting back and waiting, after you've completed the first three steps, is an action step in itself. There's a huge difference between making things happen and allowing them to happen.

As you start taking action, you'll need to choose one activity over another or one strategy over another. You'll notice that this has become more difficult due to the more personal nature of your decisions. The business is now part of you, and it's tough to separate it from your emotions. But now it's necessary (and in your best interests) to make even more rational, "Vulcan" decisions. One of the best ways I know to accomplish this is to identify the decision you're making, brainstorm all sorts of creative choices, then rank the choices from most to least desirable. Ranking your choices is crucial since you need to identify your criteria in choosing a course of action.

The choice and weighting of criteria should be strongly driven by your personal success measurements. If you want alignment between what you want and what you get, you need to make day-to-day decisions that move you toward your goals. The act of making more conscious decisions will help you achieve success right now, because you'll be following your own personal barometer and making choices that are in line with who you are.

As you make decisions that are intended to start or grow your business, you'll find that many of the things you want are not available. Look at these barriers or tests as ways to discover better, cheaper, faster ways to accomplish your goal. Ask why you want what you want. Ask "What will this thing do for my business?" and search for a better, cheaper, faster way to get what you want.

As you get deeper into running your life in a way that is more in line with who you are, you'll begin to hear things like, "This is not like you." The irony is that you might be more like yourself now than you've ever been! We are all pressured to follow a consistent and certain path most of our lives, which typically leaves some part of us undernourished, either our poet or warrior. You're learning that it's all right to be both, it's all right to nurture both, and you're probably more like yourself now than you've ever been.

Doing It Better

You've allowed yourself to make the leap. You've defined your own success measurements and have begun taking action and making decisions that will lead you to true success. Many perceived barriers have come up along the way, and you've found ways to accept these barriers as opportunities to find a better way. You are now beginning to balance your life in a directional if not precise manner.

Get ready for a shift in your development. The problems are getting bigger and the stress is coming harder and faster. You built this company to avoid all this! As intense and significant events come your way, you'll have a tendency to see them as either "good" or "bad." Resist this tendency. Realize that an event is neither good nor bad—it just is what it is.

Events take on an entirely different meaning when viewed over time and in connection with other events. If you need evidence of this, look back at your life. Think of events that either seemed all good or all bad, and think about how they played out over time.

By now you've realized that some major blocks to what you want are opportunities to rethink solutions. Think about the how of a situation, about the attitude that allows you to truly enjoy the process instead of focusing only on the result. The process of building a business is wonderful—don't taint it by categorizing every event as "good" or "bad."

When you feel stress, realize that part of being a balanced and peaceful entrepreneur is accepting stress with open arms and using it as an opportunity to test your skills, your resolve, your ability to take positive action to fix a problem or remove the source of your stress.

Realizing that business can be conducted in concert with your desire for a more loving and compassionate life is not only rewarding, it's good business. Caring enough about each human you touch, your customers, your employees, your suppliers to make decisions out of love, is a ruthless business strategy. No other competitor or alternate employee can compete with someone who really approaches their business with loving compassion, for sure it will be difficult but you'll have the edge!

Finally, realize that each decision you make in accordance with your own personal life goals is an act of heroism. No matter how small or insignificant it may seem, celebrate your own heroism and that of those around you.

Chapter 13

Heroes: A Fond Farewell to You, the Reader

If you're leading your life according to your own personal success measurements, you're a hero.

I don't have a lot of respect for talent. Talent is genetic. It's what you do with it that counts.

—Martin Ritt

As a society, we tend to look at heroes as our benchmarks. As a corporate type, I looked up to Bill Gates, Chip Conley (Joie de Vivre Hotels), Richard Branson, and Bill Marriott. Others look up to movie stars, models, singers, or musicians.

Michael Jordan is also a star. But how many people drive around in a $100,000 car, are protected by bodyguards, are set financially for life, receive standing ovations when they walk in the door, and get paid millions to endorse stuff—all for doing something that most of us would pay to do or do for free on our own time? People say, "I met Michael Jordan, and he was so nice." Well, of course he is! He's blessed with genes that help him perform as an athlete at a level few humans will ever approach. He's handsome. He has endorsements for millions of dollars. People treat as if he were an ancient god come to life. He has hundreds of "handlers" all around him. Under the same circumstances, we'd all be "nice"!

Now, I think the world of Michael Jordan, and I admire what he's done. But let me tell you, as an entrepreneur, who my other heroes are: cops, firefighters, my parents, you, me.

Think about it: we show up every day to do our jobs, earn our paychecks by doing things that people pay us to do because no one would do it for free. We have days when our cars won't start in the morning and we still get the kids to school, work all day, take the dog to the vet, pick the kids up from school, make dinner, help the kids study, clean up the kitchen, do a load of laundry, and put the kids to bed. We do it all (or most of it) with a smile on our faces, and many of us somehow find time to give our energy, resources, and hearts to charitable causes, too. This is all done quietly, without fanfare, without endorsements, without help from "handlers." You tell me: whose life is really harder? Who are the real heroes here?

This isn't a motivational speech, it's your life. As for the athletes, movie stars, rock stars—we forget that these people are here to entertain us, because we are the heroes. What you do every day with a smile on your face makes you a hero. There is heroism in the shift from employee to self-employed:

From home, from work, even from your own mind comes the appeal to keep being the one you've been. Don't change.

Do the old, familiar thing again. Just as this point in life when you feel drawn toward new beginnings, there are these powerful inner and outer forces blocking the way. The dream is your life.

—William Bridges

My dad was a recovering alcoholic. For more than 30 years, he battled with the ravages of this brutal disease. When he was 50, he fell asleep in his small home in Wisconsin and his cigarette ash burned his house down. All his clothes, his money, his personal possessions, even his eyeglasses were burned. The neighbors called my sister Nancy and described my dad standing outside in the drizzle, disconnected, not quite able to see, not quite sober, watching his house burn.

My sister quickly drove up from Chicago. When she reached our dad, she realized that even beyond the traumatic experience of the fire, his health had deteriorated dangerously. She brought him to a veterans hospital, where he was diagnosed with alcohol poisoning. His lack of adequate nourishment had stripped his system to the point where he was admitted into what they call the "death watch" unit.

My father met with his doctor the next day. Everything he had was gone: he was divorced from his wife, the only clothes he had were the ones on his back and those Nancy pulled from the Salvation Army clothing bin, and the doctor said he was probably dying.

The hospital staff spent the next several weeks nourishing my father and bringing him back to health. When it was time for him to go to a halfway house, his cravings for alcohol were still pursuing him with a vengeance. My father asked the doctor what would happen if he took a drink, and the doctor calmly responded, "Oh, you'll die." At that moment my dad chose life. He made the heroic decision—for himself and his family—to rebuild his life from ground up while fighting his own personal demons. He did it: he's been sober for 25 years now. In fact, he did so well that, as he says "I was such a good student, they made me the teacher", and he began counseling other addicts.

Several years ago, he mentioned that he couldn't remember something due to short-term memory loss from alcoholism. I said, "It's hell getting older," and he replied, "It's heller not gettin' older." Even then, he still chose life.

Our attitudes are what make us heroic. Heroism is a personal choice, not a genetic gift. Give me anything that is earned, not God-given or genetics like intellect or beauty— give me attitude, style, grace. All the personal choices people make to "do the right thing" are what should be celebrated on television, not physical appearance, luck, or athletic ability.

Life shrinks or expands in proportion to one's courage.

—Anais Nin

My mom grew up in a blue-collar household and dropped out of high school. Of Polish descent, she worked as a house-keeper when she needed money to keep her kids in school. A few years ago, she called and asked me if I could block out a certain Friday evening in about four weeks—and she wouldn't tell me why. When the date came, I drove to a community college on the South Side of Chicago and saw my mom sitting on stage with 15 other people. I began to realize what was happening. The dean of the school approached the podium and said, "We're not Harvard here, but what we do is more important." This was the graduation ceremony for a high-school GED program. My mom, in her 60's, had quietly studied for this degree and never told anyone for fear she might not reach her goal. When one of the students got up and sang "Somewhere Over the Rainbow," I realized that the greatest heroes I had ever seen were up on that stage at that moment. I was honored to sit alongside them.

There's heroism in everything you do. There's heroism in starting, growing, and managing your own business. There's heroism in redefining yourself and having the confidence to define and attain your own personal and private success measurements. You are a hero for taking the steps toward attaining the goal of entrepreneurship. It's not about the business. It's about you and a very courageous personal choice.

KEY POINTS:

Heroic behavior is a series of courageous personal decisions. Every time you reach for a life that is right for you, heroism occurs—regardless of how attractive or smart you are.

By accepting the idea that I am the effect of a subtle buffering between hereditary and societal forces, I reduce myself to a result. I am living a plot written by my genetic code, ancestral heredity, traumatic occasions, parental unconsciousness, societal accidents.

—James Hillman, The Soul's Code

Which attitude is yours? It's your choice.

About the Author

Brian Dietmeyer

Brian Dietmeyer grew up in the south side of Chicago. His father ran a local tavern and mom was a housekeeper. Brian has held positions as laborer for ironworkers and carpenters, drove a dump truck and was an assistant auto mechanic. He started his career with Marriott hotels as an assistant bartender with a high school diploma and left as a Vice President of National Account Sales. Over the course of 10 years of night and weekend education he completed his liberal arts degree at De Paul University and MBA at the Kellogg School at Northwestern.

He co-founded Think! Inc. in 1996 with Dr. Max Bazerman of the Harvard Business School. (www.e-thinkinc.com). Since then Think! has consulted in 47 countries with companies such as FedEx, Microsoft, Alcatel-Lucent, Fujitsu, Coca-Cola and American Airlines.

Brian has produced a play and managed bands at his part time and non-for profit artist management firm, ACME Garage.

www.poetandwarrior.com

http://twitter.com/poetandwarrior

brian@poetandwarrior.com

Your Epitaph

www.ingramcontent.com/pod-product-compliance
Lightning Source LLC
Chambersburg PA
CBHW071013040426
42443CB00007B/754